# Diving & Snorkelling Guide to
# TROPICAL MARINE LIFE
## OF THE INDO-PACIFIC REGION

# Diving & Snorkelling Guide to
# TROPICAL MARINE LIFE
## OF THE INDO-PACIFIC REGION

**AUSTRALIA • INDIA • INDONESIA • MALAYSIA • MALDIVES
MAURITIUS • MELANESIA • MICRONESIA • PHILIPPINES
SEYCHELLES • SINGAPORE • SRI LANKA • THAILAND • VIETNAM**

MATTHIAS BERGBAUER and MANUELA KIRSCHNER

CONSULTANT: LAWSON WOOD

# Contents

# Introduction

The abundance of different forms and species found in coral reefs gives them a biological richness equalled only by that of the tropical rainforests, providing a home for innumerable living creatures. Despite many years of exploration, marine biologists are always discovering new species in the world's coral reefs.

One of the reasons for this diversity is the reef-building hard corals. The individual animals are very small and have a very simple structure. Each is surrounded by a limestone skeleton and continuously deposits calcium at its basal plate, so the limestone base beneath the polyps is in a state of constant growth. In this way they form reefs – colonies of countless individual animals that can be several metres across. Over many generations and thousands of years, this continuous accumulation builds up into massive coral reefs, the largest structures on earth created by living beings. This is an outstanding achievement for such minute 'master builders'. During the day, hard corals appear to be lifeless, the polyps usually being visible only at night, when they extend their tentacles in order to catch plankton.

A garden beneath the waves: A floral wrasse (*Cheilinus chlorourus*) swims through the abundant landscape of the reef.

# Introduction

Almost without exception, reef-building hard corals have a second food source in addition to the plankton they catch: they live in a close symbiotic relationship with microscopic algae. These 'zooxanthellae' live inside the cells of the polyps, where they carry out photosynthesis. Polyps and algae live as part of a nutrient exchange that benefits both partners. This mutual diet supplementation, with its highly effective recycling of nutrients, makes corals extremely productive. As a result they grow rapidly despite the relatively low level of nutrients in the tropical oceans where they live.

Reef-building hard corals need very specific environmental conditions, and this limits their ability to spread. Because of their symbiotic relationship with the zooxanthellae, they require plenty of sunlight. In clear water, there is usually sufficient light for photosynthesis only up to around 50 m.

A good location: A group of feather stars makes use of an exposed coral rock to catch plankton.

Temperature is also critical. With very few exceptions, coral reefs are able to thrive only where the average temperature of the water does not fall below 20 °C. Another factor affecting coral growth is a high level of sediment: if the coral becomes covered with sand, it cannot survive. The sediment carried by major rivers, for example, means that coral reefs cannot live in areas influenced by estuarial flow.

In total, tropical coral reefs cover only about 0.015 per cent of the ocean surface, but their importance is far greater than this suggests. About one-quarter of all saltwater fish depend on coral reefs in one way or another, and almost every class of animal is represented there. This huge diversity within a small area makes coral reefs one of the most complex and fascinating environments in the world.

Master builders: These massive coral reefs are made by minute coral polyps.

# Introduction

Togetherness: Table corals shelter symbiotic algae (left); clownfish live in symbiosis with anemones (right).

The Indian and Pacific Oceans, referred to jointly as the Indo-Pacific, contain around 92 per cent of the world's coral reefs. The region includes such well-known destinations as the Red Sea, the Indian Ocean with the Maldives and the Seychelles, then further east to South-east Asia with Thailand, Indonesia and the Philippines, then on to the Western Pacific with Australia and the archipelagos of Micronesia, Melanesia and Polynesia. All the species described in this book live in the Indo-Pacific.

Every time we dive or snorkel in a coral reef, a wealth of species is not all we see: we can also observe many interesting behaviour patterns. There are astonishing survival strategies that make use of camouflage and deception, tricks and ruses, but there are also a striking number of close bonds formed between different species. The various types of symbiosis are especially interesting. Among the best known are those between clownfish and their host anemones, the ecologically vital cleaning procedures carried out by some wrasses and shrimps in partnership with hundreds of fish species, and the coexistence of many small crustaceans with a variety of reef-dwellers, such as pistol shrimps with partner gobies.

Swarms: Anthias often form large groups.
They swim close to the reef to catch plankton.

Diving on a coral reef is particularly rewarding at night, providing a completely different experience from the more familiar daytime view. Most fish rest for the night in holes and crevices, leaving the stage free for the invertebrates, who remain hidden during the day. These include numerous crustaceans, sea urchins, snails, feather stars, brittle stars, cuttlefish and squid. The changeover from day to night is almost like a change of shift in the animal world.

Finally, a coral reef is always sure to provide surprises, because it is often visited by other ocean creatures – hunting for food, visiting the cleaner stations or simply passing through. Encounters with sea turtles, for example, are not unusual on many reefs. If you are lucky and your timing is right you might also see large fish such as eagle rays and manta rays, a range of sharks, including whale sharks, or mammals such as dolphins.

Search party: Powder-blue surgeonfish and convict fish patrol the reef
in search of edible algae.

—Fishes

**NURSE SHARKS—ORECTOLOBIFORMES**
Apart from the whale shark, all other members of this group live on the seabed. They are generally harmless to humans if left undisturbed.
**WHALE SHARK** This is the largest fish of all, but despite its size and its mouth of up to 130 cm in width it feeds harmlessly on plankton. It holds its mouth wide open and moves unhurriedly along, straining large volumes of water for plankton and catching small fish and crustaceans in the process. Whale sharks are often accompanied by other fish, including jacks, cobias and remoras.
**LEOPARD SHARK** This unmistakable shark rests on the seabed during the day and goes in search of food at night, both on the reef and in nearby sandy areas. It eats molluscs and gastropods, crustaceans and bony fish. This species is also known as the zebra shark because the juveniles are striped.
**NURSE SHARK** Nurse sharks have barbels that contain taste sensors that help them to find their food. They feed at night on octopus, crustaceans, fish, sea urchins and sea snakes. They crush hard-shelled animals using their powerful jaws.

**1** | **Whale shark** *Rhincodon typus*
—Whale sharks Rhincodontidae

**GER**—Walhai  I  **FR**—Requin baleine

**LENGTH** 1,200 cm
**BIOLOGY** Active both day and night, relatively bold. Juveniles in small groups, adults mainly individually; 1–130 m.
**DISTRIBUTION** Circumtropical

**2** | **Leopard shark** *Stegostoma fasciatum*
—Leopard sharks Triakidae

**GER**—Zebrahai  I  **FR**—Requin zèbre

**LENGTH** Maximum 350 cm
**BIOLOGY** Frequently on sand and gravel close to reefs. Juveniles rarely seen, and thought to live below 50 m; 1–65 m.
**DISTRIBUTION** Red Sea to Samoa

**3** | **Tawny nurse shark** *Nebrius ferrugineus*
—Nurse sharks Ginglymostomatidae

**GER**—Gewöhnlicher Ammenhai  I  **FR**—Requin nourrice fauve

**LENGTH** 320 cm
**BIOLOGY** Often territorial if undisturbed. Usually rests in caves or under ledges during the day; 1–70 m.
**DISTRIBUTION** Red Sea to French Polynesia

**BULL SHARKS—CARCHARHINIDAE**
Bull sharks, also known as man-eating sharks, are fast, agile swimmers.
The individuals illustrated here are typical reef-dwellers and a frequent
sight in many areas
The **BLACKTIP REEF SHARK** can be encountered even in the 10-m zone.
It often hunts over the reef top, when its dorsal fin may stick out of the
water. Young sharks in particular may swim at knee depth. The **WHITETIP
REEF SHARK** also patrols its territory during the day, but tends to be more
active at night. It normally rests during the day – individually, in pairs or in
small groups – at a regular spot, perhaps under a ledge or in a cave, but
also on open sand in deeper water. These sharks can live for at least 25
years. The **GREY REEF SHARK** is territorial and has an extensive home
water area. In the pecking order of the reef it is the dominant species,
outranking blacktip and whitetip reef sharks. It hunts for bony fish such as
moray eels, soldierfish and surgeonfish, and preys on cephalopods and
large crustaceans.

**1** | **Blacktip reef shark** *Carcharhinus melanopterus*
—Bull sharks Carcharhinidae

**GER**—Schwarzspitzen-Riffhai  |  **FR**—Requin à pointes noires

**LENGTH** 180 cm
**BIOLOGY** Individually or in groups; timid; eats reef fish and squid;
0–75 m.
**DISTRIBUTION** Red Sea to French Polynesia

**2** | **Whitetip reef shark** *Triaenodon obesus*
—Bull sharks Carcharhinidae

**GER**—Weißspitzen-Riffhai  |  **FR**—Requin à pointes blanches

**LENGTH** 180 cm
**BIOLOGY** Eats reef fish and squid. Will force itself into even narrow
crevices in search of prey. Non-aggressive, timid; 1–330 m.
**DISTRIBUTION** Red Sea to Panama

**3** | **Grey reef shark** *Carcharhinus amblyrhynchos*
—Bull sharks Carcharhinidae

**GER**—Grauer Riffhai  |  **FR**—Requin gris de récif

**LENGTH** 180 cm
**BIOLOGY** Lives in outer reef slopes and reef channels, likes strong-current
areas; sometimes exhibits threatening behaviour in the Pacific; 1–275 m.
**DISTRIBUTION** Red Sea to Easter Island

# Rays

RAYS—BATOIDEI
Rays are cartilaginous fish with a flattened, disc-shaped body. Most are typical bottom-dwellers and can be seen even in very shallow sandy areas. It is also not unusual for them to bury themselves, with only their eyes and breathing holes visible. They swim using wave-like movements of their body edges, usually staying close to the seabed.
**FLYING ACES** The devilfish, eagle rays and cownose rays are different. They have abandoned their bottom-dwelling habits and can swim for long periods with great elegance, 'flying' with wing-like movements of their broad triangular pectoral fins through open water over long distances. The manta ray is a plankton filter feeder and is the largest of all the rays at 1.5 tonnes.
**SWORDSMEN** Unlike the harmless giants above, stingrays have one or more venomous stings on the top of their tails – a potent defensive weapon.

## 1 | Spotted eagle ray *Aetobatus narinari* —Eagle rays Myliobatidae

**GER**—Gefleckter Adlerrochen  I  **FR**—Aigle de mer-léopard

**LENGTH** 230 cm across
**BIOLOGY** Individually, in pairs or in schools of up to 200; visits reefs, where it burrows in the sand for molluscs and crustaceans; 1–80 m.
**DISTRIBUTION** Circumtropical

## 2 | Manta ray *Manta birostris* —Manta rays and Devil rays Mobulidae

**GER**—Manta  I  **FR**—Raie manta océanique

**LENGTH** Up to 670 cm across
**BIOLOGY** Individually or in groups of up to 50; regularly seen on reefs, where it also visits cleaner stations; 1–50 m.
**DISTRIBUTION** Circumtropical

## 3 | Thurston's devil ray *Mobula thurstoni* —Manta rays and Devil rays Myliobatidae

**GER**—Thurstons Teufelsrochen  I  **FR**—Mante vampire

**LENGTH** Up to 180 cm across
**BIOLOGY** Pelagic, also close to reefs. Swims singly or in groups. Filters zooplankton from the water. There are two very similar species.
**DISTRIBUTION** Circumtropical

1
2
3

## 1 Porcupine ray *Urogymnus asperrimus*
—Stingrays Dasyatidae

**GER**—Igelrochen  I  **FR**—Raie porc-épic

**LENGTH**  100 cm across
**BIOLOGY**  Inhabits sheltered reef areas, rests on sand, gravel and seagrass beds. Active both day and night; burrows for prey, including crustaceans, worms and wrasses; 1–120 m.
**DISTRIBUTION**  Red Sea and East Africa to Marshall Islands, Great Barrier Reef and Fiji

## 2 Black-spotted stingray *Taeniura meyeni*
—Stingrays Dasyatidae

**GER**—Schwarzpunkt-Stechrochen  I  **FR**—Pastenague à taches noires

**LENGTH**  164 cm across
**BIOLOGY**  Sand and gravel reef areas; eats fish and invertebrates that live on the seabed; non-aggressive, though fatal incidents have occurred when divers attempted to ride the animals; 3–500 m.
**DISTRIBUTION**  Red Sea to Galápagos

## 3 Kuhl's stingray *Dasyatis kuhlii*
—Stingrays Dasyatidae

**GER**—Kuhls Stechrochen  I  **FR**—Pastenague à points bleus

**LENGTH**  50 cm across
**BIOLOGY**  A common species on sand or mud surfaces, typically close to the reef. Frequently covers itself with sand, making it difficult to spot. Eats invertebrates living in the sand; 0.5–90 m.
**DISTRIBUTION**  South Africa to Samoa

### 1 | **Pink whipray** *Himantura fai*
—Stingrays Dasyatidae

**GER**—Fais Stechrochen  |  **FR**—Raie fouet

**LENGTH**  Disc width 150 cm
**BIOLOGY**  Prefers sand and gravel areas in lagoons and outer reefs.
Usually solitary, sometimes in groups; 1–200 m.
**DISTRIBUTION**  South Africa, Maldives, India to north-west Australia,
Mariana Islands and Tuamotus in French Polynesia

### 2 | **Blue-spotted stingray** *Taeniura lymma*
—Stingrays Dasyatidae

**GER**—Blaupunkt-Stechrochen  |  **FR**—Raie pastenague à taches bleues

**LENGTH**  35 cm across
**BIOLOGY**  Sand and gravel reef areas. Visits cleaner stations. Active by
day and night; scrabbles in the seabed for molluscs and worms; often rests
during the day under ledges and table corals; 2–30 m.
**DISTRIBUTION**  Red Sea to Fiji

### 3 | **Leopard torpedo** *Torpedo panthera*
—Torpedo rays Torpedinidae

**GER**—Panther-Torpedorochen  |  **FR**—Torpille panthère

**LENGTH**  100 cm long
**BIOLOGY**  Mostly on sand; not rare but usually buried. Uses electric shocks
from its pair of specialized organs to stun bottom-dwelling fish including
scorpionfish; 0.5–55 m.
**DISTRIBUTION**  Red Sea and Gulf of Aden

**MORAY EELS—MURAENIDAE**

Moray eels look frightening but are not aggressive. The few accidents reported are mostly the result of feeding, threatening or harpooning them. Morays accustomed to being fed lose their fear and may become intrusive. The regular opening and closing of the mouth is not a threatening gesture but a breathing mechanism. When the mouth is closed, inhaled water rich in oxygen is pumped across the gills and expelled through the small gill opening at the back of the head.

**A GOOD NOSE** During the day they stay in holes and crevices, often peeking out slightly from their hiding places. At night they prowl the reef looking for prey, relying mainly on their acute sense of smell due to poor eyesight. Species with sharp fangs eat mainly fish, while those with tapered teeth eat crustaceans, sea urchins and snails.

**1** | **Giant moray** *Gymnothorax javanicus*
—Moray eels Muraenidae

**GER**—Riesenmuräne   I   **FR**—Murène géante

**LENGTH**  230 cm
**BIOLOGY**  Eats fish and young whitetip reef sharks; occasionally crustaceans and octopus; 1–46 m.
**DISTRIBUTION**  Red Sea to Panama

**2** | **Honeycomb moray** *Gymnothorax favagineus*
—Moray eels Muraenidae

**GER**—Große Netzmuräne   I   **FR**—Murène léopard

**LENGTH**  220 cm
**BIOLOGY**  Active by day and night; relatively bold. As well as on reefs, it is sometimes found in open seaweed meadows; 1–50 m.
**DISTRIBUTION**  Southern Red Sea to Samoa

**3** | **Fimbriated moray** *Gymnothorax fimbriatus*
—Moray eels Muraenidae

**GER**—Gelbkopf-Muräne   I   **FR**—Murène à tête jaune

**LENGTH**  80 cm
**BIOLOGY**  Hunts at night for fish and crustaceans, so more often seen at night than during the day; timid and nervous; 1–50 m.
**DISTRIBUTION**  Seychelles, Maldives to French Polynesia

1
2
3

## 1 | Blackcheek moray *Gymnothorax breedeni*
—Moray eels Muraenidae

**GER**—Bartmuränen  |  **FR**—Murène à joues noires

**LENGTH**  120 cm
**BIOLOGY**  Lives in outer reef slopes with strong currents; do not approach too closely – this species may be aggressive and can bite very quickly; 4–25 m.
**DISTRIBUTION**  Comores, Seychelles, Maldives to French Polynesia

## 2 | Whitemouth moray *Gymnothorax meleagris*
—Moray eels Muraenidae

**GER**—Weißmaulmuräne  |  **FR**—Murène à bouche blanche

**LENGTH**  120 cm
**BIOLOGY**  The white interior of the mouth gives it a distinctive appearance; active by day and night, feeds mainly on fish and crustaceans; 0.3–36 m.
**DISTRIBUTION**  Red Sea to Galápagos Islands

## 3 | Geometric moray *Gymnothorax griseus*
—Moray eels Muraenidae

**GER**—Graue Muräne  |  **FR**—Murène tatouée

**LENGTH**  65 cm
**BIOLOGY**  Lives in rock and coral reefs; common species, frequently seen during the day among seaweed and gravel; juveniles often shelter in groups of up to 10; 1–30 m.
**DISTRIBUTION**  Red Sea to West Indies

**1** | **Ribbon moray** *Rhinomuraena quaesita*
—Moray eels Muraenidae

**GER**—Geister-Muräne  |  **FR**—Murène ruban

**LENGTH** 120 cm
**BIOLOGY** Changes sex from male to female during growth: juveniles are black; males (65 cm and over) are blue and yellow; females (94 cm and over) are yellow; 1–57 m.
**DISTRIBUTION** East Africa to French Polynesia

**2** | **Starry moray** *Echidna nebulosa*
—Moray eels Muraenidae

**GER**—Sternfleckenmuräne  |  **FR**—Murène étoilée

**LENGTH** 75 cm
**BIOLOGY** From tidal zone to 30 m depth. May briefly leave the water to catch crustaceans on rocky shores. Juveniles are more often found in tidal pools on the reef top. This species often goes hunting in open areas at night; 0–30 m.
**DISTRIBUTION** Red Sea to south-west Japan and French Polynesia

**3** | **Zebra moray** *Gymnomuraena zebra*
—Moray eels Muraenidae

**GER**—Zebra-Muräne  |  **FR**—Murène zébrée

**LENGTH** 150 cm
**BIOLOGY** Solitary, lives in crevices and overhangs of exposed reef tops and outer reef slopes. Solitary; often seen peering from its shelter. Feeds mainly on crustaceans and also on molluscs and sea urchins; 1–50 m.
**DISTRIBUTION** Red Sea to Hawaii and French Polynesia

SNAKE EELS—OPHICHTHIDAE
The snake eel family consists of approximately 290 species, though they are rarely seen by divers.
**UNDERGROUND** Most species spend their lives buried in sand or soft sediment with only their heads or eyes visible above the surface. Divers see them most frequently at night. Often confused with sea snakes, they are in fact bony fish, their closest relatives being the moray eels. Most species have a hard, narrowly tapering tail, which they use to dig themselves very quickly backwards into the sand or sediment. They can even retreat under the sand. Some types have similar colouring to sea snakes, but they are easily distinguished: sea snakes have visible scales, whereas snake eels are smooth-skinned. They also have fin membranes and pectoral fins, which sea snakes do not.

## 1 | **Marbled snake eel** *Callechelys marmorata* —Snake eels Ophichthidae

**GER**—Marmor-Schlangenaal  I  **FR**—Anguille-serpent marbrée

**LENGTH** 85 cm
**BIOLOGY** Easily identified by its white or cream background with distinct, evenly-distributed black spots. Uncommon despite its wide distribution. Lives in sandy reef zones and adjacent sediment surfaces. Hunts at night for small fish and crustaceans, using its sense of smell to guide it; 3–25 m.
**DISTRIBUTION** Red Sea to French Polynesia

## 2 | **Napoleon snake eel** *Ophichthus bonaparti* —Snake eels Ophichthidae

**GER**—Bonaparte-Schlangenaal  I  **FR**—Anguille-serpent Napoléon

**LENGTH** 75 cm
**BIOLOGY** Easily recognized by its attractively patterned head. The rest of its body, marked with wide dark-coloured stripes, resembles that of the sea snake. Lives in fine to coarse sand on coastal and outer reefs, and in lagoons. Occasionally seen at night in open water. An ambush predator of small fish and squid. May bite in self-defence; 1–20 m.
**DISTRIBUTION** East Africa to French Polynesia

**EELTAIL CATFISHES—PLOTOSIDAE**
There are over 3,000 species of catfish, but most of them live in fresh water. Those that live in the sea include the Striped eel catfish – the only one seen with any frequency by divers and snorkellers, depending on location. It eats bottom-dwelling species such as crustaceans and molluscs, and fish, which it detects using the barbels around its mouth. During the breeding season the male sets up a nest beneath a rock, where he guards the eggs.

**1** | **Striped eel catfish** *Plotosus lineatus*
— Eeltail catfishes Plotosidae

**GER**—Gestreifter Korallenwels  I  **FR**—Poisson-chat rayé

**LENGTH** 33 cm
**BIOLOGY**  Lives in lagoons, coastal reefs and seaweed meadows. The juveniles form dense, spherical groups ('catfish balls'), which are kept together by scent (pheromones). Adults live individually or in small groups. Avoid approaching these fish: their pectoral and ventral fins have stings that can cause severe – in rare cases dangerous – poisoning; 1–60 m.
**DISTRIBUTION**  Red Sea to Samoa

**LIZARDFISHES—SYNODONTIDAE**
These small ambush predators with large mouths and numerous sharp teeth are common in most areas. Divers who approach carefully may get very close, but the fish often dart away at the last moment and resettle a few metres off. Lying motionless on sand or gravel, rock or coral, they dart forward to capture tiny fish, which they swallow whole.

**2** | **Two-spot lizardfish** *Synodus binotatus*
— Lizardfishes Synodontidae

**GER**—Zweifleck-Eidechsenfisch  I  **FR**—Anoli à deux taches

**LENGTH** 13 cm
**BIOLOGY** Lizardfish, including this species, are able to change colour to match their background, as their spotted pattern makes them easily overlooked. Their variable colouring makes them difficult to distinguish among the various but rather similar species on the reef: in this species, the two black dots on the tip of the nose help to identify it; 1–30 m.
**DISTRIBUTION**  Gulf of Aden, Maldives to Hawaii and Tonga

# Frogfishes

FROGFISHES—ANTENNARIIDAE
Despite being brightly coloured, frogfishes are very well camouflaged: they blend perfectly into their surroundings or they resemble sponges. They can change colour over several days if necessary.

**HOAXER** On its upper lip, the frogfish has a movable fishing rod with what looks like fleshy 'bait' at the end. Predators lured by this apparent snack often swim directly in front of its mouth.

**FAST FOOD** The frogfish opens its mouth and sucks in prey with astonishing speed: just six thousandths of a second – a world record! No other vertebrate can seize its prey so quickly.

**SLOW MOTION** The frogfish uses its pectoral and ventral fins to walk over the ground in two different ways – a step-by-step motion or a gallop, the latter being the slowest in the animal kingdom. It swims for short distances using the principle of jet propulsion, drawing water into its mouth and expelling it through nozzle-shaped gills. Its jet 'engine', too, is the slowest of any vertebrate.

## 1 | Giant frogfish *Antennarius commersoni*
—Frogfishes Antennariidae

**GER**—Riesen-Anglerfisch  |  **FR**—Grenouille de Commerson

**LENGTH** 30 cm
**BIOLOGY** The largest species. Highly variable in colour – white, yellow, pink, red, orange, greenish, brown and black are known. The fish are frequently the same colour all over, but sometimes have flecks of other colours with a crusted appearance. Often found under ledges, and very fond of living among sponges. Individually or in pairs; 1–70 m.
**DISTRIBUTION** Red Sea to Panama

## 2 | Painted frogfish *Antennarius pictus*
—Frogfishes Antennariidae

**GER**—Rundflecken-Anglerfisch  |  **FR**—Laffe cochon

**LENGTH** 21 cm
**BIOLOGY** A highly variable species, with local colour variants and possibly subspecies, making identification difficult. Its skin texture allows it to mimic sponges, including the inlet and outlet openings (see photograph). Often found on sponges, also on living coral, gravel, and sand or sediment. Also eats lionfish; 1–70 m.
**DISTRIBUTION** Red Sea to French Polynesia

**SOLDIERFISHES AND SQUIRRELFISHES—HOLOCENTRIDAE**
**RED GUARD** The colour red dominates in most species of this family, which is divided into two subfamilies: soldierfishes and squirrelfishes. All species have large eyes and clearly visible scales. The most obvious differences are the squirrelfish's head, which tapers to a point, and the large spike on its gill covers; soldierfish have more rounded heads and no spike, or only a very small one.
**NOCTURNAL** These fish are active mainly at night, which is why they have large, light-sensitive eyes. However, despite being nocturnal, they are readily seen at close quarters during the day, when they wait, moving gently in the shelter of caves, ledges or beneath table corals. Species may be seen individually, in small groups or forming dense shoals. They leave their refuges at night, when soldierfishes hunt for zooplankton in open water. Squirrelfishes feed on bottom-dwelling species such as crustaceans, worms and even small fish.

**1** | **Sabre squirrelfish** *Sargocentron spiniferum*
— Soldierfishes and Squirrelfishes Holocentridae

**GER**—Großdorn-Husar  I  **FR**—Lion baroque

**LENGTH** 45 cm
**BIOLOGY** The largest species; spends the day under ledges; relatively bold and allows divers to approach closely; 1–122 m.
**DISTRIBUTION** Red Sea to Hawaii and Australia

**2** | **White-tip soldierfish** *Myripristis vittata*
— Soldierfishes and Squirrelfishes Holocentridae

**GER**—Weißspitzen-Soldatenfisch  I  **FR**—Soldat à bord blanc

**LENGTH** 20 cm
**BIOLOGY** Spends the day under ledges, primarily on outer reef slopes, often in large, tight concentrations; 15–80 m.
**DISTRIBUTION** East Africa to French Polynesia

**3** | **Spotfin squirrelfish** *Neoniphon sammara*
—Soldierfishes and Squirrelfishes Holocentridae

**GER**—Blutfleck-Husar  I  **FR**—Écureuil tacheté

**LENGTH** 32 cm
**BIOLOGY** Common species, relatively bold. Often seen moving across staghorn corals and between rocks; 2–45 m.
**DISTRIBUTION** Red Sea to Hawaii and French Polynesia

**CORNETFISHES—FISTULARIIDAE**

The extremely elongated cornetfish stalks small fish, taking them by surprise and grabbing them with a sudden dart forward. Its narrow, tube-shaped snout means it can catch only relatively small prey, sucking them in, pipette-like. It can change colour within seconds, from silvery green to pale or dark greyish brown.

## 1 | **Cornetfish** *Fistularia commersonii*
—Cornetfishes Fistulariidae

**GER**—Flötenfisch  |  **FR**—Poisson-flûte

**LENGTH**  150 cm

**BIOLOGY**  Patrols the reef individually or in loose groups. Feeds on small fish and crustaceans. Sometimes swims 'piggyback', concealed behind a larger fish to approach prey unnoticed; occasionally does the same with divers; 1–128 m.

**DISTRIBUTION**  Red Sea to Panama

**TRUMPETFISHES—AULOSTOMIDAE**

Closely related to the cornetfish, trumpetfish use the same hunting method, including the tactic of swimming close to other fish to approach prey unawares. Juveniles and adults have different colouring. Individuals are able to modify their colour pattern; a yellow (xanthic) variant also occurs in some regions.

## 2 | **Trumpetfish** *Aulostomus chinensis*
—Trumpetfishes Aulostomidae

**GER**—Trompetenfisch  |  **FR**—Poisson-trompette chinois

**LENGTH**  80 cm

**BIOLOGY**  Usually seen individually, sometimes also in loose pairs. Sometimes adopts a vertical posture among horn corals for camouflage. The trumpetfish family consists of only two species: in addition to the Indo-Pacific species illustrated here (**2a** and **2b**), another species occurs in the Atlantic that lives in the Atlantic, including the Caribbean; 1–122 m.

**DISTRIBUTION**  South Africa to Panama

## NEEDLEFISHES—BELONIDAE

Needlefish are very elongated predators with a pointed snout and numerous needle-like teeth. They live in surface waters, catch small fish and are very well camouflaged with their silvery-blue colouring. To evade their enemies they are able to catapult themselves out of the water at remarkable speed.

**1** | **Crocodile houndfish** *Tylosurs crocodilus*
—Needlefishes Belonidae

**GER**—Krokodil-Hornhecht  |  **FR**—Orphie crocodile

**LENGTH**  135 cm
**BIOLOGY**  Lives in coastal waters; usually swims just below the surface; leaps from the water and skids across the surface using its tail fin; the largest species in its family. Sometimes jump towards fishing lights at night, and have caused injuries to anglers and fishermen. Underwater they are placid.
**DISTRIBUTION**  Circumtropical

## SEAMOTHS—PEGASIDAE

These small bottom-feeding fish get their name from their wing-like pectoral fins, though they move mainly by creeping across the seabed. Their armoured bodies restrict movement to the tail only. They feed on minute invertebrates. When disturbed they spread out their pectoral fins like wings.

**2** | **Little dragonfish** *Eurypegasus draconis*
—Seamoths Pegasidae

**GER**—Zwerg-Flügelrossfisch  |  **FR**—Dragon de mer

**LENGTH**  8 cm
**BIOLOGY**  Lives in sheltered areas such as lagoons and quiet coves, on sand, mud and gravel, often buried. Occasionally seen in pairs during the mating season. Colouring varies depending on background: whitish against light coloured sand to dark brown; 1–90 m.
**DISTRIBUTION**  Red Sea to French Polynesia

1
2

# Ghost Pipefishes

**GHOST PIPEFISHES — SOLENOSTOMIDAE**
Only five species are known in this small, intriguing family. They are very well camouflaged and are thus often overlooked. Even when a diving guide points out a feather star, it usually takes a while before divers spot the ornate ghost pipefish being indicated. Finding these fish is often like searching for a needle in a haystack. Because of this secretive lifestyle, the fifth species was not discovered and described by marine biologists until 2002.

**INCUBATORS** Females grow larger than males and, unlike related pipefishes and seahorses, they incubate the eggs. To this end, the females' ventral fins form a brood pouch capable of holding several hundred eggs. The eggs hatch after 10–20 days into transparent larvae. Ghost pipefishes feed on tiny shrimps and amphipods, which they suck into their long tubular mouths.

## 1   Robust ghost pipefish *Solenostomus cyanopterus*
—Ghost pipefishes Solenostomidae

**GER**—Seegras-Geisterpfeifenfisch   I   **FR**—Poisson-fantôme robuste

**LENGTH** 15 cm
**BIOLOGY** Colouring variable: green, yellow, grey or dark brown. Resembles seaweed, and the brown varieties usually have light-coloured speckles that look like the encrusted growths on dead seaweed. They can wave to and fro like dead leaves of seaweed in the current. Usually in pairs on sand, between algae and seaweed; 0.2–20 m.
**DISTRIBUTION** Red Sea to Fiji

## 2   Ornate ghost pipefish *Solenostomus paradoxus*
—Ghost pipefishes Solenostomidae

**GER**—Harlekin-Geisterpfeifenfisch   I   **FR**—Poisson-fantôme orné

**LENGTH** 11 cm
**BIOLOGY** Has numerous grotesque skin appendages; colour variable: background colour often red, yellowish or almost black with white or yellow markings. Usually lives in the shelter of feather stars, horn or black corals. Most often swims at an angle with its head downwards; often seen in pairs, occasionally also in small groups; 2–30 m.
**DISTRIBUTION** Red Sea to Fiji

**SEAHORSES—SYNGNATHIDAE**
Seahorses are among the strangest of finned creatures, as they scarcely resemble fish. Their scaleless skin is protected by bony rings. Seahorses swim slowly, moving through the water with gentle movements of their dorsal fins. They possess a long prehensile tail that coils tightly, and they often use it to grip on to seaweed, horn coral or other vegetation. The tail also acts as a rudder when the seahorse is swimming.
**ROLE REVERSAL** It is the male seahorse who is responsible for incubating the eggs. Reproduction begins with a prolonged, intricate courtship ritual that can last up to three days, after which the female lays up to 150 eggs (depending on species) in the brood pouch of the male. The eggs are then fertilized in the pouch by the male, and incubated for several weeks. When the young fish finally hatch out from the eggs, the male expels them with strong pumping movements into the water through a small opening in the brood pouch.

## 1 | **Common seahorse** *Hippocampus kuda*
—Seahorses Syngnathidae

**GER**—Kuda-Seepferdchen  |  **FR**—Hippocampe d'estuaire

**LENGTH** 15 cm
**BIOLOGY** Shallow coastal reefs, also in seaweed, estuaries, harbours and brackish water. Colouring is variable: not only yellow but also dark brown to black; 2–55 m.
**DISTRIBUTION** India to Hawaii and French Polynesia

## 2 | **Pygmy seahorse** *Hippocampus bargibanti*
—Seahorses Syngnathidae

**GER**—Zwerg-Seepferdchen  |  **FR**—Hippocampe nain de Bargibant

**LENGTH** 2 cm
**BIOLOGY** Lives on muricella horn coral, where the tubercles on its skin look like the closed coral polyps. If it is on gorgonian coral (*M. paraplectana*) it has orange tubercles, while on red coral (*M. plectana*) it has red ones (see photograph). Photograph (right): perfect camouflage, shown life-size; 15–50 m.
**DISTRIBUTION** South Japan, the Philippines, Indonesia, North Australia; possibly elsewhere

1
2

## PIPEFISHES — SYNGNATHIDAE

Pipefishes and seahorses together form a single family. They feed on bottom-dwelling invertebrates and zooplankton, and some of the larger species also eat young fish, though these must be very small. Pipefishes have no teeth, so they suck in prey through their pipette-shaped mouths and swallow them whole.

**1** | **Network pipefish** *Corythoichthys flavofasciatus*
— Pipefishes Syngnathidae

**GER**—Netz-Seenadel  |  **FR**—Syngnathe à traits jaunes

**LENGTH** 15 cm
**BIOLOGY** The male pipefish incubates the eggs, which are transferred to the male's underbelly after a prolonged courtship ritual. In some species the eggs lie in a protective skin fold; in others they remain exposed and readily visible on the male's belly. The eggs hatch after about four weeks; 1–25 m.
**DISTRIBUTION** Red Sea to Maldives

## SNIPEFISHES — CENTRISCIDAE

This family contains only four species, of which two are deep-sea fishes. The other two are a regular sight on reefs, depending on region. Their sharp ventral keel, composed of bony plates, gives them the name razorfish. They use their toothless pipette-like mouths to suck up plankton from the water.

**2** | **Coral razorfish** *Aeoliscus strigatus*
— Snipefishes Centriscidae

**GER**—Gestreifter Schnepfenmesserfisch  |  **FR**—Poisson-couteau

**LENGTH** 15 cm
**BIOLOGY** Swims close to the bottom, sometimes in schools of up to a hundred, always in a vertical, head-downward posture. The fish only swim horizontally when fleeing from danger, and they quickly revert to the vertical position. Often found upside-down among bushy horn corals or sheltered by long-spined sea urchins; 0.5 to at least 20 m.
**DISTRIBUTION** Aldabra and Seychelles to New Caledonia

1
2

# Lionfishes

**LIONFISHES—PTEROINAE**

Lionfishes are conspicuous, flamboyant fish. They often proceed slowly, almost majestically, across the reef, or they float gently on the spot with minimal movement. They are relatively bold and will sometimes approach even to within touching distance of a diver who remains still.

**DANGEROUS BEAUTY** Many of the conspicuous fin spines are venomous. Although no deaths have been reported and the venom is not as dangerous as has sometimes been alleged, it can cause intense pain and envenomation, and divers can easily be injured when trying to scare away fish that have approached them. If the fish feel threatened they can suddenly sting with outspread spines, so the best response is to move away if the fish get too close. Lionfishes use their venom for defence, not for catching prey. They prey on small fish and crustaceans. A typical hunting method is to drive smaller fish into a corner, where they then use their enlarged pectoral fins to trap them.

## 1 | Common lionfish *Pterois miles*
—Lionfishes Pteroinae

**GER**—Indischer Rotfeuerfisch | **FR**—Poisson-scorpion commun

**LENGTH** 38 cm

**BIOLOGY** Often close to ledges and caves, or in wrecks. Hunts at dusk and during the night for fish, prawns and shrimps. Opens out its pectoral fins to drive its prey into a corner. Found individually or in small groups; 1–60 m.

**DISTRIBUTION** Red Sea to Bali and Sumbawa. The closely related red lionfish (*P. volitans*) is found from the Gulf of Thailand to the Pitcairn Islands

## 2 | Spotfin lionfish *Pterois antennata*
—Lionfishes Pteroinae

**GER**—Antennen-Feuerfisch | **FR**—Poisson-scorpion à antennes

**LENGTH** 20 cm

**BIOLOGY** Common species, easily recognized by its long, freely moving pectoral fin spines, which are joined at the base by a black-spotted membrane. Usually found under ledges and in hollows. Individually or in small groups. Inactive during the day; hunts for shrimps and prawns during late afternoon and at night; 1–50 m.

**DISTRIBUTION** East Africa; Maldives to French Polynesia

1
2

**1** | **Shortfin lionfish** *Dendrochirus brachypterus*
—Lionfishes Pteroinae

**GER**—Kurzflossen-Feuerfisch | **FR**—Ptérois à courtes nageoires

**LENGTH** 15 cm
**BIOLOGY** Lies in wait for prey, usually at the base of freestanding coral blocks or rocks; individually or in harems with up to 10 females; 2–80 m.
**DISTRIBUTION** Red Sea to Samoa

**2** | **Mombasa lionfish** *Pterois mombasae*
—Lionfishes Pteroinae

**GER**—Mombasa-Feuerfisch | **FR**—Ptérois de Mombasa

**LENGTH** 19 cm
**BIOLOGY** Pectoral fin spines with a dark-spotted membrane. Prefers areas with soft coral and sponges on deep outer reef slopes; 10–60 m, rarely above 20 m.
**DISTRIBUTION** Red Sea (rare) to Papua New Guinea

**3** | **Twinspot lionfish** *Dendrochirus biocellatus*
—Lionfishes Pteroinae

**GER**—Zweifleck-Feuerfisch | **FR**—Ptérois ocellé

**LENGTH** 10.5 cm
**BIOLOGY** Eye spots on the dorsal fin. Lives in coral-rich reefs. Timid, hides during daylight hours. Hunts at night and is normally only seen at that time; 1 m to at least 40 m.
**DISTRIBUTION** Mauritius to Society Islands

**SCORPIONFISHES—SCORPAENINAE**
Scorpionfishes are typical bottom-dwellers and spend most of their time on the seabed. They have a rudimentary swim bladder and are very reluctant to swim, and do so for no more than a few metres before sinking down to the bottom again.
**RAPID STRIKE BEHAVIOUR** Despite their ponderous appearance, they can dart forwards with extraordinary speed, and belong to the fast-movers of the fish world. Ambush predators, they wait motionless and well-camouflaged for any prey that passes close by. Then, their lethargy vanishes and they suddenly shoot forwards, open their large mouths in a flash, and suck in their unwary victims. Scorpionfishes have venomous fin spines, which explain their name. However, they do not use their spines to catch prey but only for their own defence. Their venom is painful for humans but not usually dangerous.

## 1 | Tasselled scorpionfish *Scorpaenopsis oxycephala*
—Scorpionfishes Scorpaeninae

**GER**—Fransen-Drachenkopf  |  **FR**—Poisson-scorpion à houppes

**LENGTH** 36 cm
**BIOLOGY** Like other species it is capable of changing its colour in a matter of seconds to match its background; 1–43 m.
**DISTRIBUTION** Red Sea to Great Barrier Reef

## 2 | Devil scorpionfish *Scorpaenopsis diabolus*
—Scorpionfishes Scorpaeninae

**GER**—Buckel-Drachenkopf  |  **FR**—Poisson-scorpion diable

**LENGTH** 30 cm
**BIOLOGY** Frequently confused with the stonefish; if disturbed, reveals the coloured inner surface of its pectoral fins; 1–70 m.
**DISTRIBUTION** Red Sea to Hawaii and French Polynesia

## 3 | Leaf scorpionfish *Taenianotus triacanthus*
—Scorpionfishes Scorpaeninae

**GER**—Schaukelfisch  |  **FR**—Rascasse feuille

**LENGTH** 12 cm
**BIOLOGY** Very variable in colour; sways sideways to resemble a leaf moving in the swell of the sea; 1–134 m.
**DISTRIBUTION** East Africa to Galápagos Islands

STONEFISHES — SYNANCEINAE

Take care – this is the most venomous fish known. Its venomous fin spines are for defence only, but the fish are not at all timid and not easily deterred. The danger for divers is accidentally treading on a stonefish or brushing up against one. Although their venom is rarely fatal, it is extremely painful.

**1** | **Reef stonefish** *Synanceia verrucosa*
—Stonefishes Synanceinae

**GER**—Echter Steinfisch  |  **FR**—Poisson pierre commun

**LENGTH**  38 cm

**BIOLOGY**  Stonefishes are masters of disguise, and live up to their 'stony' name. Their hunting strategy is to sit and wait. They can remain motionless in one place for days on end. When an unsuspecting fish comes within reach, the predator opens its enormous mouth with lightning speed and sucks in its victim; sometimes several fish all lie together (three fish are shown in the photo); 0.3–45 m.

**DISTRIBUTION**  Red Sea to French Polynesia

DEVILFISHES — CHORIDACTYLINAE

Their very name spells trouble. Devilfishes do indeed have highly venomous fin spines. They live on sand or gravel, and often bury themselves right up to the eyes and wait for passing prey. They swim rarely, preferring to crawl by means of their claw-like pectoral fin rays along the substrate.

**2** | **Spiny devilfish** *Inimicus didactylus*
—Devilfishes Choridactylinae

**GER**—Finger-Teufelsfisch  |  **FR**—Poisson-démon

**LENGTH**  19 cm

**BIOLOGY**  When at rest, the devilfish closes its pectoral fins and folds its caudal fin towards the body. This gives it excellent camouflage and makes it difficult to see. When it is threatened it opens out the pectoral fin and raises its tail fin so that its brilliant colours act as a warning. It can shed its skin every few months; 5–40 m.

**DISTRIBUTION**  Andaman Sea to Vanuatu

1

2

WASPFISHES—TETRAROGIDAE

Waspfishes are related to scorpionfishes and, like them, have venomous fin spines. Their most striking feature is the dorsal fin, which starts on the head in front of the eyes. Most live on soft substrates. There are at least 28 species, found in shallow, tropical waters in the Indo-Pacific.

**1** | **Cockatoo waspfish** *Ablabys taenianotus*
—Waspfishes Tetrarogidae

**GER**—Kakadu-Stirnflosser  |  **FR**—Laffe de fond

**LENGTH**  15 cm
**BIOLOGY**  Colour variable, yellow to chocolate-brown; face and body are sometimes different, contrasting colours. Moves across the substrate using pectoral fins. Lives on sheltered sand, mud and gravel areas, individually or in pairs. Rolls over sideways to disguise itself as a dead leaf.
**DISTRIBUTION**  Andaman Sea (Thailand) to Fiji and south-east Australia

FLATHEADS—PLATYCEPHALIDAE

Flatheads are typical bottom-dwellers and have no swim bladder. During the day, many of these ambush predators burrow into the sandy seabed to camouflage themselves. To do this they lie on the ground and make lateral shaking movements with their whole body. The sand they have stirred up then settles evenly all over them.

**2** | **Tentacled flathead** *Papilloculiceps longiceps*
—Flatheads Platycephalidae

**GER**—Gemeiner Krokodilsfisch  |  **FR**—Poisson-crocodile tapis

**LENGTH**  100 cm
**BIOLOGY**  Often more or less completely covered in sand. Relatively bold. Catches shrimps, prawns and fish. It can also use a 'vertical take-off' movement to catch fish swimming a couple of metres above the seabed. Its eyes have reticulated, size-adjustable eye lappets to protect them against UV radiation.
**DISTRIBUTION**  Red Sea to Oman; a very similar species is found as far as French Polynesia

1

2

**FLYING GURNARDS—DACTYLOPTERIDAE**
Flying gurnards use their modified ventral fins to creep across the seabed.
They spread out their huge, fan-like pectoral fins if disturbed, and can then
move forwards a short distance and glide a little way using the rigid
extended pectoral fins. They cannot, however, 'flap' their wings.

**1** | **Oriental flying gurnard** *Dactylopterus orientalis*
—Flying gurnards Dactylopteridae

**GER**—Helm-Knurrhahn   |   **FR**—Grondin volant oriental

**LENGTH**  38 cm
**BIOLOGY**  Solitary species living on sandy substrates in lagoons and
sheltered outer reef slopes. It is an impressive sight when gliding with its
outspread pectoral fins. When the fins are folded down, however, it is
relatively well camouflaged, especially if part-buried. It is able to create
sounds by using its swim bladder as a resonance chamber.
**DISTRIBUTION**  Red Sea to French Polynesia

**STARGAZERS—URANOSCOPIDAE**
These club-shaped fish have eyes that sit on top of their heads and point
upwards (hence the name 'stargazer'), and a wide, horizontal mouth
opening. However, what appear to be teeth are really skin fringes on their
lips. Some species, including all *Uranoscopus* species, have a worm-shaped
flap of skin, which can be extended or retracted, on their lower jaw. This
acts as a lure to attract small fish, which the stargazer seizes by rapidly
opening its mouth.

**2** | **Whitemargin stargazer** *Uranoscopus sulphureus*
—Stargazers Uranoscopidae

**GER**—Gefleckter Sterngucker   |   **FR**—Uranoscope à bordure blanche

**LENGTH**  Approximately 35 cm
**BIOLOGY**  Lives on sand and mud, in lagoons and sheltered outer reef
slopes. An ambush predator, it typically buries itself in the ground, often
leaving only its eyes and lips exposed, and lies in wait for passing prey.
To attract its prey it is able to wave a worm-shaped extension on its
lower jaw.
**DISTRIBUTION**  Red Sea to Samoa

1

2

## TILEFISHES—MALACANTHIDAE

These very elongated fish live close to the seabed in sandy or gravel substrates adjacent to reefs. They are seen frequently, but only from a distance, as they are very timid and alert. If danger threatens they immediately escape into burrows they have made. Tilefishes eat bottom-dwelling invertebrates, or take zooplankton from the current.

**1** | **Flagtail tilefish** *Malacanthus brevirostris*
—Tilefishes Malacanthidae

**GER**—Gestreifter Torpedobarsch  |  **FR**—Poisson couvreur

**LENGTH**  30 cm
**BIOLOGY**  Individually or (mainly juveniles) in groups. Very timid, not easily approached, but in some areas it is a very common representative of this small tropical fish family. Like other tilefishes it lays its eggs inside its nest burrow; the eggs are guarded by both parents; 5–61 m.
**DISTRIBUTION**  Red Sea to Panama

## SUCKERFISHES—ECHENEIDAE

The primary dorsal fin of these fish has been modified to form a distinctive grooved suction disc. The fish use this like a suction cup to create a vacuum, which they use to cling on to larger creatures, which then carry them along. They attach themselves to various shark species, rays, large bony fish and whales, and even dugongs, turtles and ships. This small family is made up of eight species.

**2** | **Sharksucker** *Echeneis naucrates*
—Suckerfishes Echeneidae

**GER**—Gestreifter Schiffshalter  |  **FR**—Rémora commun

**LENGTH**  110 cm
**BIOLOGY**  Lives in open seas but comes to reefs with its respective host, as it is often found on sharks, rays and sometimes even turtles. Feeds on small fish, sometimes also on the prey of its host, and takes parasites from the host's surface. More frequent reef visitors are juveniles without a host – they sometimes try to attach themselves to divers! 1–60 m.
**DISTRIBUTION**  All tropical and subtropical seas

1

2

## SOAPFISHES—GRAMMISTINAE

This small subfamily within the seabass group (Serranidae) gets its name from its mucous-covered skin. It produces a bitter-tasting venom called grammistin, which seems to protect the fish from both predators and skin parasites. Many soapfishes are nocturnal and hide in caves and crevices during the day.

**1** | **Sixline soapfish** *Grammistes sexlineatus*
—Soapfishes Grammistinae

**GER**—Sechsstreifen-Seifenbarsch  I  **FR**—Mérou à rayures d'or

**LENGTH**  27 cm
**BIOLOGY**  Lives on reef tops, in lagoons and on outer reef slopes with caves and crevices. Also lives in brackish water. Juveniles are common but are usually concealed in hiding places. Adults move to deeper waters of up to 150 m, although they are also found at 1–40 m.
**DISTRIBUTION**  Red Sea to French Polynesia

## LONGFINS—PLESIOPIDAE

The comet is the most widespread of the roughly 20 species in this family, and is a favourite in marine aquaria thanks to its attractive colouring. However, comets in general are rare. Species in the genus *Assessor* are mouth breeders: the male incubates the eggs in his mouth until they hatch.

**2** | **Comet** *Calloplesiops altivelis*
—Longfins Plesiopidae

**GER**—Augenfleck-Mirakelbarsch  I  **FR**—Comète à grandes nageoires

**LENGTH**  20 cm
**BIOLOGY**  Relatively common and widespread, but lives in hiding inside crevices. Timid, emerging only at sunset. Its white spots become more numerous and smaller with age; 3–45 m.
**DISTRIBUTION**  Red Sea to French Polynesia

1

2

**DOTTYBACKS—PSEUDOCHROMIDAE**
Dottybacks are a family of small but highly colourful species. Most belong to the genus *Pseudochromis* and are timid, living in concealment within crevices and reef shelters. They are seldom seen by divers even though they are not rare. All species hold small territories, which they defend aggressively.

**1** | **Sunrise dottyback** *Pseudochromis flavivertex*
—Dottybacks Pseudochromidae

**GER**—Gelbblauer Zwergbarsch | **FR**—Pseudochromis à dos jaune

**LENGTH** 7 cm
**BIOLOGY** The males are blue with a broad yellow stripe at the top, while the females are entirely yellow, and live a more concealed life so are rarely seen. Usually lives in sandy or gravel areas at the base of reef blocks. Timid and cautious, but frequently moves several metres away from its base.
**DISTRIBUTION** Red Sea, Gulf of Aden

**BIGEYES—PRIACANTHIDAE**
Their red colouring and, above all, their large eyes are indicators of their nocturnal lifestyle. During the day they often float without moving in sheltered spots such as ledges. In some areas, notably in the Maldives, they are also frequently seen in large groups out in the open, close to the seabed.

**2** | **Crescent-tail bigeye** *Priacanthus hamrur*
—Bigeyes Priacanthidae

**GER**—Riff-Großaugenbarsch | **FR**—Gros yeux commun

**LENGTH** 40 cm
**BIOLOGY** Often on outer reef slopes, typically in the vicinity of shelters such as caves and crevices. Individually or in small, informal groups, not particularly timid. Nocturnal; eats zooplankton in open water. Able to change colour instantly from bright red to silver flecks to uniform pale silver; 10 m to more than 100 m.
**DISTRIBUTION** Red Sea to French Polynesia

1

2

ANTHIAS—ANTHIINAE

**EYE-CATCHING** Anthias are relatively small but are magnificently coloured in many shades of red, violet, orange and yellow. They also form large groups – sometimes huge accumulations of more than 2,000 fish. These dense, pulsating masses in constant movement are one of nature's most impressive spectacles.

**MULTIPLE MATES** Always staying close to the reef, these agile diurnal fish catch zooplankton in open water. When disturbed they swim towards the reef, where they seek shelter from danger, and also at night, in crevices in the coral. They live in harems. Depending on the species, each male can have several females and even as many as 30. The males are slightly larger and develop from high-status females by a sex-change process. When they change sex they also develop new and brighter colouring.

## 1 | Scalefin anthias *Pseudanthias squamipinnis* —Anthias Anthiinae

**GER**—Juwelen-Fahnenbarsch  |  **FR**—Anthias commun

**LENGTH** 15 cm
**BIOLOGY** Forms large, frequently conspicuous groups in front of reef crests, steep slopes and drop-offs. The male of this species has an elongated dorsal fin ray, and guards a harem of between 5 and 10 females; 0.3–35 m.
**DISTRIBUTION** Red Sea to Fiji and southern Japan

## 2 | Yellowback anthias *Pseudanthias evansi* —Anthias Anthiinae

**GER**—Gelbrücken-Fahnenbarsch  |  **FR**—Anthias bicolore

**LENGTH** 10 cm
**BIOLOGY** Commonly on outer reef slopes. Forms small groups, sometimes also larger shoals, but always stays close to or only 1–2 m above the substrate; up to 40 m.
**DISTRIBUTION** East Africa to Mauritius, Andaman Sea and Christmas Island

## 3 | Square-spot fairy basslet *Pseudanthias pleurotaenia* —Anthias Anthiinae

**GER**—Rechteck-Fahnenbarsch  |  **FR**—Anthias à tache carrée

**LENGTH** 20 cm
**BIOLOGY** Forms loose groups, predominantly on steep outer reef slopes. Males with a harem of up to eight females; 10–180 m.
**DISTRIBUTION** Bali to south-west Japan, Great Barrier Reef, New Caledonia and Samoa

GROUPERS—SERRANIDAE

**CLOSE TO HOME** Groupers are solitary and territorial. Most of these powerful bottom-feeding fish live on coral reefs and rocky seabeds, where the rough texture of the terrain gives them perfect cover. Their territories include sheltered hiding places such as caves, crevices and ledges, and here they spend a large part of the day. However, some patrol the reef more or less in the open, even during the day.

**SURPRISE TACTICS** All groupers are predators, and are one of the largest and most common predator species on the reef. They feed mainly on crustaceans, fish and squid, and their best hunting period is at twilight. In spite of their rather stout appearance, groupers can dart forwards with astonishing speed, and can seize, from a standstill, fish that are faster and more agile than themselves. Pursuit, on the other hand, is not their primary strategy, and offers them little chance of success.

## 1 | **Coral grouper** *Cephalopholis miniata* — Groupers Serranidae

**GER**—Juwelen-Zackenbarsch  |  **FR**—Vieille étoilée

**LENGTH** 40 cm
**BIOLOGY** Common, relatively bold. Prefers large, coral-rich lagoons and outer reef slopes; 1–50 m.
**DISTRIBUTION** Red Sea to French Polynesia

## 2 | **Saddle grouper** *Cephalopholis sexmaculata* — Groupers Serranidae

**GER**—Sechsstreifen-Zackenbarsch  |  **FR**—Vieille à six taches

**LENGTH** 50 cm
**BIOLOGY** Lives in clear coastal and outer reefs, mostly spends the day in caves. Adopts a head-down posture on reef tops or walls; 3–150 m.
**DISTRIBUTION** Red Sea to French Polynesia

## 3 | **Peacock hind** *Cephalopholis argus* — Groupers Serranidae

**GER**—Pfauen-Zackenbarsch  |  **FR**—Vieille cuisinier

**LENGTH** 55 cm
**BIOLOGY** Prefers coral-rich reefs, likes to rest in sheltered places on hard substrates. Adults often in pairs or small groups. Can quickly lighten or darken its colouring; 1–40 m.
**DISTRIBUTION** Red Sea and East Africa to south-west Japan and French Polynesia

**1** **Blacktip grouper** *Epinephelus fasciatus*
—Groupers Serranidae

**GER**—Baskenmützen-Zackenbarsch  I  **FR**—Mérou oriflamme

**LENGTH** 40 cm
**BIOLOGY** Like the other species, its colouring depends greatly on the background: pale cream to deep reddish-brown; 1–160 m.
**DISTRIBUTION** Red Sea to French Polynesia

**2** **Potato grouper** *Epinephelus tukula*
—Groupers Serranidae

**GER**—Kartoffel-Zackenbarsch  I  **FR**—Mérou patate

**LENGTH** 200 cm
**BIOLOGY** Prefers clear, coral-rich areas. Individually or in small groups. Mostly rare, only seen in a few places; allows divers to come very close and occasionally hand-feed them; 3–150 m.
**DISTRIBUTION** Red Sea to Great Barrier Reef

**3** **Malabar grouper** *Epinephelus malabaricus*
—Groupers Serranidae

**GER**—Malabar-Zackenbarsch  I  **FR**—Mérou malabare

**LENGTH** 120 cm
**BIOLOGY** Regionally uncommon. Lies in wait in reef channels or at the base of the reef above sand and gravel; eats crayfish, fish and squid. Timid and cautious, a valued edible fish; 2–100 m.
**DISTRIBUTION** Red Sea to Tonga

1
2 
3

## 1 | Slender grouper *Anyperodon leucogrammicus*
—Groupers Serranidae

**GER**—Spitzkopf-Zackenbarsch  |  **FR**—Mérou élégant

**LENGTH** 52 cm
**BIOLOGY** In lagoons and outer reef slopes with plentiful growth of coral. Solitary, eats fish. Usually found in sheltered areas. The juveniles' pattern mimics the longitudinally striped *Halichoeres labrid* fish, in order to get closer to their prey; 2–50 m.
**DISTRIBUTION** Red Sea and East Africa to south-west Japan, Samoa and Great Barrier Reef

## 2 | Roving coral grouper *Plectropomus pessuliferus marisrubi*
—Groupers Serranidae

**GER**—Rotmeer-Forellenbarsch  |  **FR**—Mérou loche vagabonde

**LENGTH** 110 cm
**BIOLOGY** Common in the Red Sea. Patrols the reef slowly, also during the day. The Panther grouper (*P. p. pessuliferus*) is its closely related subspecies found from the Indian Ocean to Fiji; 3–50 m.
**DISTRIBUTION** Red Sea

## 3 | Yellow-edged lyretail *Variola louti*
—Groupers Serranidae

**GER**—Mondsichel-Zackenbarsch  |  **FR**—Mérou croissant de lune

**LENGTH** 80 cm
**BIOLOGY** Patrols the reef slowly, also during the day. A prowling predator, it attempts to get very close to its prey. Common, relatively bold. Juveniles are a different colour and live in hiding; 1–150 m.
**DISTRIBUTION** Red Sea to French Polynesia

HAWKFISHES—CIRRHITIDAE
**A SEAT WITH A VIEW** Hawkfishes swim rarely, and then only for very short distances. They are ground-based and have no swim bladder. Most of the time they perch on a preferred vantage point, resting on their powerful pectoral fins. They like to do this on exposed coral promontories, which gives them their other popular name, the coral watchman. The name 'hawkfish' is likewise related to this habit. Like a bird of prey, they keep watch on their surroundings from a perch, diving down rapidly on passing prey – mainly shrimps and small fish.
**SEX CHANGE** Hawkfishes are protogynous hermaphrodites: they initially reach sexual maturity as females, but can later change into males if necessary. The male then often builds up a harem of several females, which he actively guards.

## 1 | **Freckled hawkfish** *Paracirrhites forsteri*
—Hawkfishes Cirrhitidae

**GER**—Forsters Büschelbarsch | **FR**—Épervier de Forster

**LENGTH** 22 cm
**BIOLOGY** Colour variable, typically marked with small dark spots on the head. Feeds mainly on small fish and shrimps; 1–40 m.
**DISTRIBUTION** Red Sea to Polynesia

## 2 | **Arc-eye hawkfish** *Paracirrhites arcatus*
—Hawkfishes Cirrhitidae

**GER**—Monokel-Büschelbarsch | **FR**—Épervier strié

**LENGTH** 14 cm
**BIOLOGY** Typically on small, branched coral colonies such as *Pocillopora* and *Stylophora*. Eats small crustaceans; 1–35 m.
**DISTRIBUTION** East Africa, Maldives to Polynesia

## 3 | **Longnose hawkfish** *Oxycirrhites typus*
—Hawkfishes Cirrhitidae

**GER**—Langnasen-Büschelbarsch | **FR**—Épervier à nez long

**LENGTH** 13 cm
**BIOLOGY** Usually lives in gorgonian or black coral. Its 'tartan' pattern and snout are unmistakable. Eats plankton, crustaceans; 5–70 m.
**DISTRIBUTION** Red Sea to Panama

**CARDINALFISHES—APOGONIDAE**
Cardinalfishes are small fish, rarely more than 12 cm in length. Most species are active at twilight and after dark. They are slow swimmers, and live close to the seabed in a small territorial area. During the day they float quietly, preferably in cracks, among branched corals. Sometimes they stay out in the open, but always close to a coral block or a rock. At twilight they leave their hiding places. Most of them then hunt for zooplankton, while others also eat small fish and bottom-dwelling crustaceans. The tiger cardinalfish has large fangs and feeds mainly on fish.
**MOUTH PROTECTION** In the *Apogon* species, mating is preceded by a courtship ritual. After spawning, the fertilized eggs are collected by the male and incubated in his highly extendible mouth cavity for approximately one week. Here the eggs are protected from predators and are aerated by water rich in oxygen. During this very effective incubation period the male takes no food.

**1** | **Ring-tailed cardinalfish** *Apogon aureus*
| —Cardinalfishes Apogonidae

**GER**—Sonnen-Kardinalbarsch  I  **FR**—Apogon doré

**LENGTH** 12 cm
**BIOLOGY** Active by day, in sheltered reefs, often in large groups close to shelter; 1–40 m.
**DISTRIBUTION** East Africa, Maldives to Tonga

**2** | **Five-lined cardinalfish** *Cheilodipterus quinquelineatus*
| —Cardinalfishes Apogonidae

**GER**—Fünflinien-Kardinalbarsch  I  **FR**—Apogon à cinq lignes

**LENGTH** 12 cm
**BIOLOGY** In small groups close to hiding places among coral or rocks, or sheltering in long-spined sea urchins; 1–40 m.
**DISTRIBUTION** Red Sea to French Polynesia

**3** | **Tiger cardinalfish** *Cheilodipterus macrodon*
| —Cardinalfishes Apogonidae

**GER**—Tiger-Kardinalbarsch  I  **FR**—Apogon à grandes dents

**LENGTH** 25 cm
**BIOLOGY** Floats individually or in small groups in the shelter of caves or ledges. Common, relatively bold; 0.5–40 m.
**DISTRIBUTION** Red Sea to French Polynesia

## JACKS—CARANGIDAE

Jacks are skilled hunters of the open sea, but they are regularly seen by divers since many species like to spend time close to the coast and to reefs. **HIGH-SPEED PREDATORS** These nimble predators are active by day and night, and are constantly on the move. They have to do this because they have only a rudimentary swim bladder, and would sink if they stayed still. Their narrow tailstock with a deeply forked caudal fin shows that they are untiring, high-speed hunters. Fish are at the top of their menu, and sometimes it is possible to see and admire the impressive speeds they reach when hunting. Some species circle slowly in shoals in open water close to the reef. Many of these silver predators are sought-after edible species, and in some places they are very important commercially. Juveniles of some species make use of jellyfish as protection when they are out in open sea that is otherwise devoid of shelter. Young golden trevally are also well known as 'pilot fish' because they accompany sharks, among other species.

### 1 | Giant trevally *Caranx ignobilis* —Jacks Carangidae

**GER**—Dickkopf-Makrele  |  **FR**—Carangue géante

**LENGTH**  170 cm
**BIOLOGY**  Individually or in small groups, often on patrol in front of escarpments; juveniles in schools; 5–80 m.
**DISTRIBUTION**  Red Sea to French Polynesia

### 2 | Orange-spotted trevally *Carangoides bajad* —Jacks Carangidae

**GER**—Zitronen-Stachelmakrele  |  **FR**—Carangue lentigine

**LENGTH**  53 cm
**BIOLOGY**  Often in small groups at regular spots towards the top of the reef by day; yellow variant common in the Red Sea; 1–90 m.
**DISTRIBUTION**  Red Sea to Indonesia

### 3 | Golden trevally *Gnathanodon speciosus* —Jacks Carangidae

**GER**—Gold-Makrele  |  **FR**—Carangue têtue

**LENGTH**  110 cm
**BIOLOGY**  Juveniles yellow with black bars; adults in deep lagoons and on outer reef slopes; 1–50 m.
**DISTRIBUTION**  Red Sea to Panama

SNAPPERS—LUTJANIDAE
**HUNTERS** Snappers are reef-dwelling fish that remain close to the seabed, and are mostly inactive by day, when they remain individually or in small groups in sheltered places, such as under ledges. They are also frequently seen in sizeable groups near the seabed out in the open. In many reefs, these massive, stationary shoals of snappers are one of the most spectacular sights for divers. Fully-grown specimens of some of the larger species are solitary. Snappers are nocturnal predators, feeding primarily on bottom-dwelling invertebrates, especially crustaceans, and on squid, small fish and plankton species. The species that feed mainly on fish are readily recognizable by their fangs.
**HUNTED** The snapper family is a large one with more than 100 species. They are found all over the world – in tropical and sub-tropical regions and also in the Atlantic and the Caribbean. Many are important and valuable edible fish; in some areas, however, certain species can cause ciguatera poisoning, and must not be eaten.

## 1 | Humpback snapper *Lutjanus gibbus*
—Snappers Lutjanidae

**GER**—Buckel-Schnapper  I  **FR**—Vivaneau pagaie

**LENGTH** 50 cm
**BIOLOGY** Often in large, stationary shoals during the day. Hunts alone at night for crustaceans; 1–150 m.
**DISTRIBUTION** Red Sea to French Polynesia

## 2 | Bluestripe snapper *Lutjanus kasmira*
—Snappers Lutjanidae

**GER**—Blaustreifen-Schnapper  I  **FR**—Vivaneau à raies bleues

**LENGTH** 35 cm
**BIOLOGY** Individually, in small groups or in massive shoals. Hunts at night for small fish and crustaceans; 10–264 m.
**DISTRIBUTION** Red Sea to French Polynesia

## 3 | Midnight snapper *Macolor macularis*
—Snappers Lutjanidae

**GER**—Gelbaugen-Schnapper  I  **FR**—Vivaneau minuit

**LENGTH** 55 cm
**BIOLOGY** Eats mostly large zooplankton; juveniles have a striking black-and-white pattern and elongated fins; 3–50 m.
**DISTRIBUTION** Maldives to Solomon Islands

FUSILIERS — CAESIONIDAE

Fusiliers are closely related to the snappers, but live more in the open sea, where they feed on zooplankton. They therefore have a small mouth and, because of their open-water habitat, a more streamlined body with a deeply forked caudal fin. A solitary fusilier may be unremarkable, but these fish are very familiar to divers even if their name is not well known

**SHOALING BEHAVIOUR** In many areas the great shoals of fusiliers form a large proportion of the sea's abundance. By day these skilful, untiring swimmers rest in large numbers in open water. They live by the steep outer reef slopes, and also in lagoons. Being surrounded by these fish when descending or ascending is always an experience for a diver. During the night, the fish sleep on the reef, hidden in cracks and holes, and often take on a reddish nocturnal colouring. During the day, they seek out a reef, where they visit cleaner stations. Fusiliers are sought-after edible fish, and there are about 20 different species.

## 1 | **Bluestreak fusilier** *Pterocaesio tile*
—Fusiliers Caesionidae

**GER**—Neon-Füsilier  |  **FR**—Fusilier à ligne bleue

**LENGTH** 25 cm
**BIOLOGY** Hunts for zooplankton in open water, sometimes in large shoals. Rests at night in crevices and cavities, when its lower body turns red (see photograph); 5–25 m.
**DISTRIBUTION** East Africa to Polynesia

## 2 | **Red Sea fusilier** *Caesio suevica*
—Fusiliers Caesionidae

**GER**—Rotmeer-Füsilier  |  **FR**—Fusilier de Suez

**LENGTH** 25 cm
**BIOLOGY** Tail has striking black and white tips. In large shoals in open water close to reefs, feeds on zooplankton. Frequently encountered and inquisitive, will often surround divers. Visits cleaner stations; 1–25 m.
**DISTRIBUTION** Red Sea

## 3 | **Yellowback fusilier** *Caesio xanthonota*
—Fusiliers Caesionidae

**GER**—Gelbrücken-Füsilier  |  **FR**—Fusilier à dos jaune

**LENGTH** 30 cm
**BIOLOGY** Swims in large schools in the open waters of deep lagoons, and along outer reef slopes. There are several similar species with dorsal stripes of differing lengths; 0.5–50 m.
**DISTRIBUTION** Southern Red Sea, Maldives to Maluku Islands

SWEETLIPS—HAEMULIDAE
**DAYDREAMERS** During the day, sweetlips rest quietly in the water –
alone, in small groups, some also in large shoals. They show little fear, and
many species are attractively coloured. Some like to be in the open, and
even in exposed locations, while others prefer more sheltered areas and
remain beneath table corals or ledges. Many species have thick, fleshy
lips, although members of the *Haemulon* genus do not. Juveniles are
frequently a completely different colour, and some of them swim around
alone, sometimes with tumbling or rippling movements, in contrast to the
calm behaviour of the adults.
**NIGHT FEEDERS** Sweetlips become active at night, and go individually in
search of food. Their principal food is bottom-dwelling invertebrates, and
they use their molars to crush crustaceans, molluscs, snails or sea urchins.
They also eat worms and small fish. Some sweetlips also hunt for
zooplankton in open water. The family includes about 120 species, many
of which are popular edible fish.

## 1 | **Giant sweetlips** *Diagramma pictum*
—Sweetlips Haemulidae

**GER**—Silber-Süßlippe  |  **FR**—Gaterin peint

**LENGTH**  90 cm
**BIOLOGY**  A large species; lagoons and reef slopes, individually or in small
groups by day; 1–30 m.
**DISTRIBUTION**  Red Sea to Sri Lanka

## 2 | **Many-spotted sweetlips** *Plectorhinchus chaetodonoides*
—Sweetlips Haemulidae

**GER**—Harlekin-Süßlippe  |  **FR**—Gaterin arlequin

**LENGTH**  70 cm
**BIOLOGY**  In coral-rich reefs, under ledges by day. Juveniles brown with
white spots and a tumbling swimming action; 1–40 m.
**DISTRIBUTION**  Maldives to Fiji

## 3 | **Oriental sweetlips** *Plectorhinchus orientalis*
—Sweetlips Haemulidae

**GER**—Orient-Süßlippe  |  **FR**—Gaterin oriental

**LENGTH**  86 cm
**BIOLOGY**  Coral-rich outer reef slopes, adults often in small groups in
sheltered or completely open locations; 2–30 m.
**DISTRIBUTION**  East Africa to Samoa

**EMPERORFISHES — LETHRINIDAE**
Many of the species in this family are a silvery-grey colour with no obvious pattern, so they are difficult for divers to identify. Emperorfishes also have widely varying body shapes: some, for example, have a steeply sloping face, while others have a pointed head.

**QUICK CHANGE** Smaller species, such as the striped large-eye sea bream, often live in small groups, while larger fish like the yellowfin emperor are mostly solitary. In many species the adults and juveniles are markedly different in colour. They feed mainly on bottom-dwelling invertebrates such as crustaceans and worms, and also on small fish and, in some cases, plankton. Many species are able to change colour within seconds in response to environmental or behavioural stimuli, and in particular can become lighter or darker. Young humpnose big-eye bream have dark bands, which they can display or suppress.

**ACTIVE** Most species feed at night, some feed during the day, and many are active by day and night. All species are sequential hermaphrodites, reaching sexual maturity initially as females and then becoming males later in life.

## 1 | Humpnose big-eye bream *Monotaxis grandoculis* — Emperorfishes Lethrinidae

**GER**—Großaugen-Straßenkehrer  |  **FR**—Capitaine bossu

**LENGTH** 60 cm
**BIOLOGY** Common, individually or in loose groups, during the day mostly hover motionless near reef margins; 1–100 m.
**DISTRIBUTION** Red Sea to Polynesia and Sumbawa

## 2 | Striped large-eye bream *Gnathodentex aurolineatus* — Emperorfishes Lethrinidae

**GER**—Leuchtfleck-Straßenkehrer  |  **FR**—Capitaine strié

**LENGTH** 30 cm
**BIOLOGY** Common, relatively bold, spends the day mostly in small groups but also, more rarely, in large assemblies close to coral blocks; 1–30 m.
**DISTRIBUTION** East Africa to Polynesia

## 3 | Yellowfin emperor *Lethrinus erythracanthus* — Emperorfishes Lethrinidae

**GER**—Gelbflossen-Straßenkehrer  |  **FR**—Capitaine empereur

**LENGTH** 70 cm
**BIOLOGY** A visually distinctive species. Solitary, timid. Likes to spend the day under or close to a ledge. Feeds on hard-shelled invertebrates; 12–120 m.
**DISTRIBUTION** East Africa to Polynesia

**FALSE SNAPPERS—NEMIPTERIDAE**
False snappers are interval swimmers: they swim a short distance, then float motionless above the seabed, catch small invertebrates and sometimes bottom-dwelling fish, then swim a little further, scanning the ground for food, then stay still again for a while. In some areas they are an important food source.

## 1 | Bridled monocle bream *Scolopsis bilineatus*
—False snappers Nemipteridae

**GER**—Schärpen-Scheinschnapper  |  **FR**—Mamila griffée

**LENGTH** 23 cm
**BIOLOGY** Adults are solitary and live close to sandy areas in lagoons and sheltered reefs. Probably a sequential hermaphrodite like all false snappers: females can change into males later in life. The juveniles imitate the venomous fangblenny (*Meiacanthus* spp.); 1–25 m.
**DISTRIBUTION** Laccadives and Maldives to Fiji

**SEABREAM—SPARIDAE**
There are only a few seabream species in the Indo-Pacific, and they are most likely to be seen in the Indian Ocean. They are also relatively timid here and difficult to approach. They are present in far greater numbers and with more species in the Atlantic, Caribbean and Mediterranean, where they also play a greater ecological role.

## 2 | Twobar seabream *Acanthopagrus bifasciatus*
—Seabream Sparidae

**GER**—Doppelband-Meerbrasse  |  **FR**—Pagre double bande

**LENGTH** 50 cm
**BIOLOGY** A wary and timid species, but frequently seen around the Red Sea. Lives on reef slopes in deep lagoons. More common at high tide on reef tops, and likes to be on or in front of outer reef slopes with a strong swell and surf. Swims alone, or also frequently in small groups; 0.2–20 m.
**DISTRIBUTION** Red Sea, Arabian Gulf to Mauritius

1

2

**SWEEPERS—PEMPHERIDAE**
During the day they remain under ledges, in cavities, in the shelter of large coral blocks and also in wrecks – the brownish *Pempheris* species with their hatchet-shaped bodies, and the slender, transparent *Parapriacanthus* species. The latter form impressive, stationary shoals. At night they hunt individually for zooplankton in open water.

**1** | **Glassy sweeper** *Parapriacanthus ransonneti*
—Sweepers Pempheridae

**GER**—Indischer Glasfisch  I  **FR**—Poisson hachette nain

**LENGTH**  10 cm
**BIOLOGY**  Relatively bold. Feeds at night on zooplankton across the reef. During the day it is possible to observe the large, dense shoals and study the shoal behaviour of fish at close quarters. In a spectacular fashion, they move out of the way of predators or divers in a pulsating mass, often forming a hollow space and then joining up again; 0.3–40 m.
**DISTRIBUTION**  Red Sea to Marshall Islands and New Caledonia

**MOONFISHES—MONODACTYLIDAE**
The five species in this family live mainly in estuaries and mangrove regions. They are tolerant of fluctuations in salinity, and are able to survive in fresh water. They frequently swim in large schools, close to the shore and in turbid water. They feed on small fish and invertebrates. The only species likely to be seen while diving is the silver moonfish.

**2** | **Silver moonfish** *Monodactylus argenteus*
—Moonfishes Monodactylidae

**GER**—Silber-Flossenblatt  I  **FR**—Lune d'argent

**LENGTH**  22 cm
**BIOLOGY**  Resembles the batfish but is not related to it. These attractive fish live in calm waters, mainly in brackish rivers, deltas and lagoons but also in sheltered coastal reefs. Lives mostly in a school; relatively bold 0–15 m.
**DISTRIBUTION**  Red Sea to Samoa

**MULLET—MULLIDAE**
There are about 55 species of mullet, all of which have two barbels on the chin. These can be held flat in an episternal notch under the chin, while swimming for example, and are then almost invisible. The barbels are organs of touch and are densely covered with taste buds. Their purpose is to find food. Mullet search the sandy seabed with their barbels outstretched, unearthing small creatures in the ground. They frequently dig their prey out from deep in the sand. Their food sources include crustaceans, molluscs, brittle stars and fish. Some species also use their barbels as a whip to drive fish out from crevices or from between the branches of the coral.

**DINING COMPANIONS** When mullet stir up the seabed they often attract other fish, such as wrasses and emperor fishes. These fish follow the mullet and catch bottom-dwelling creatures flushed out by the agitation. Although they are the only ones to benefit from the mullet's search for food, they do no harm to the mullet. This type of relationship is known as commensalism.

## 1 | **Red Sea goatfish** *Parupeneus forsskali* —Mullet Mullidae

**GER**—Rotmeer-Barbeh  |  **FR**—Capucin à bande noire

**LENGTH** 28 cm
**BIOLOGY** Common, active by day, relatively bold. Often in the company of other fish, especially wrasses; 1–30 m.
**DISTRIBUTION** Red Sea, Gulf of Aden

## 2 | **Yellowfin goatfish** *Mulloidichthys vanicolensis* —Mullet Mullidae

**GER**—Gelbflossen-Barbe  |  **FR**—Capucin de Vanicolo

**LENGTH** 38 cm
**BIOLOGY** Common, relatively bold. Nocturnal; often spends the day in large groups on reef slopes; 1–50 m.
**DISTRIBUTION** Red Sea to Polynesia

## 3 | **Manybar goatfish** *Parupeneus multifasciatus* —Mullet Mullidae

**GER**—Vielstreifen-Barbe  |  **FR**—Capucin à trois bandes

**LENGTH** 35 cm
**BIOLOGY** Individually or in groups, mostly diurnal. Highly variable but consistently vivid colouration; 1–140 m.
**DISTRIBUTION** Cocos Islands to Hawaii and Polynesia

1
2 
3

BUTTERFLYFISHES—CHAETODONTIDAE
**BRIGHT COLOURS**  With their poster-bright colours, butterflyfish are a perfect example of vividly coloured coral fish. Their bodies are flattened laterally and are almost disc-shaped, giving them the perfect shape for manoeuvring nimbly among the coral.
**TWO BY TWO**  Many species of butterflyfish live in pairs, and in some species this bond is for life. Others that live in pairs have a looser bond and are frequently seen on their own. Finally, some butterflyfish, such as the schooling bannerfish, gather in large groups or shoals. This is thought to be a defensive behaviour: these species feed on plankton in the open water in front of a reef, and a shoal provides safety from predators.
**SOCIABLE**  Many butterflyfishes are territorial and defend their space against others of the same species. These disputes can become quite heated, but are mostly limited to ritualistic behaviour, which includes staring, darting rapidly towards each other, chasing, bolting and circling. It is rare for this to escalate into actual fighting.

## 1 | Spotted butterflyfish *Chaetodon guttatissimus* —Butterflyfishes Chaetodontidae

**GER**—Tüpfel-Falterfisch  ı  **FR**—Papillon moucheté

**LENGTH**  12 cm
**BIOLOGY**  Moves across the reef in pairs or in small groups. Its food is mainly worms, coral polyps and algae; 2–25 m.
**DISTRIBUTION**  East Africa, Maldives to western Thailand

## 2 | White collar butterflyfish *Chaetodon collare* — Butterflyfishes Chaetodontidae

**GER**—Halsband-Falterfisch  ı  **FR**—Papillon à collier blanc

**LENGTH**  16 cm
**BIOLOGY**  Relatively bold. Swims in pairs, frequently also hovering in small, stationary groups in front of coral bommies. Feeds on coral polyps and worms; 1–20 m.
**DISTRIBUTION**  Gulf of Aden, Maldives to the Philippines

## 3 | Scrawled butterflyfish *Chaetodon meyeri* — Butterflyfishes Chaetodontidae

**GER**—Schwarzstreifen-Falterfisch  ı  **FR**—Papillon de Meyer

**LENGTH**  18 cm
**BIOLOGY**  Usually in pairs, territorial. Feeds only on coral polyps. Juveniles mainly in the shelter of horn corals; 2–25 m.
**DISTRIBUTION**  East Africa, Maldives to Polynesia

**1** | **Threadfin butterflyfish** *Chaetodon auriga*
— Butterflyfishes Chaetodontidae

**GER**—Fähnchen-Falterfisch  I  **FR**—Papillon cocher

**LENGTH** 23 cm
**BIOLOGY** Common, relatively bold, widespread. Individually, in pairs or in small groups. Feeds selectively on coral polyp, small worms, anemones and algae; 1–35 m.
**DISTRIBUTION** Red Sea to French Polynesia

**2** | **Bennett's butterflyfish** *Chaetodon bennetti*
— Butterflyfishes Chaetodontidae

**GER**—Bennetts Falterfisch  I  **FR**—Papillon de Bennett

**LENGTH** 18 cm
**BIOLOGY** Individually or in pairs, prefers coral-rich lagoons and outer reef slopes. Feeds on coral polyps. Juveniles can be seen among the branches of horn corals; 5–30 m.
**DISTRIBUTION** East Africa, Maldives to Pitcairn Islands

**3** | **Melon butterflyfish** *Chaetodon trifasciatus*
— Butterflyfishes Chaetodontidae

**GER**—Rippen-Falterfisch  I  **FR**—Papillon côtelé Indien

**LENGTH** 15 cm
**BIOLOGY** Usually lives in pairs, and is territorial. An extremely specialized feeder, it eats only coral polyps; 1–20 m.
**DISTRIBUTION** East Africa, Maldives to French Polynesia

**1** | **Red-back butterflyfish** *Chaetodon paucifasciatus*
— Butterflyfishes Chaetodontidae

**GER**—Rotmeer-Winkelfalterfisch  I  **FR**—Papillon orange

**LENGTH** 14 cm
**BIOLOGY** Lives in pairs or small groups. Common and relatively bold. Maintains an extensive territory. Its preferred food is stone corals and soft corals; 1–30 m.
**DISTRIBUTION** Endemic to Red Sea and Gulf of Aden

**2** | **Masked butterflyfish** *Chaetodon semilarvatus*
— Butterflyfishes Chaetodontidae

**GER**—Masken-Falterfisch  I  **FR**—Chaetodon à demi masqué

**LENGTH** 23 cm
**BIOLOGY** Mostly in pairs, sometimes in groups. Hovers under table corals during the day, and especially before noon. Common and relatively bold; 3–20 m.
**DISTRIBUTION** Endemic to Red Sea and Gulf of Aden

**3** | **Longnose butterflyfish** *Forcipiger flavissimus*
— Butterflyfishes Chaetodontidae

**GER**—Röhrenmaul-Pinzettfisch  I  **FR**—Papillon longnez

**LENGTH** 22 cm
**BIOLOGY** Roams in pairs or small groups, mainly on outer reef slopes. Relatively bold. Wide range of food sources, also picks off the feet of sea urchins or starfish; 2–110 m.
**DISTRIBUTION** Red Sea to Central America

## 1 | Pyramid butterflyfish *Hemitaurichthys polylepis*
— Butterflyfishes Chaetodontidae

**GER**—Gelber Pyramiden-Falterfisch  |  **FR**—Poisson-papillon pyramide jaune

**LENGTH**  18 cm
**BIOLOGY**  Prefers outer reef slopes exposed to current. Usually in large shoals and often quite a few metres away from the reef in order to catch zooplankton in the open water; 3–50 m.
**DISTRIBUTION**  Cocos (Keeling) and Christmas Islands to Japan, Hawaii and Pitcairn Island

## 2 | Copperband butterflyfish *Chelmon rostratus*
— Butterflyfishes Chaetodontidae

**GER**—Kupferstreifen-Falterfisch  |  **FR**—Chelmon commun

**LENGTH**  20 cm
**BIOLOGY**  Along coasts and inner reefs, also in sandy and muddy areas with turbid water. Territorial species. Solitary or in pairs. Eats invertebrates, which it extracts from small crevices with its tubular snout; 1–25 m.
**DISTRIBUTION**  Andaman Sea and north-west Australia to south-west Japan, the Philippines, Papua New Guinea and Great Barrier Reef

## 3 | Schooling bannerfish *Heniochus diphreutes*
— Butterflyfishes Chaetodontidae

**GER**—Schwarm-Wimpelfisch  |  **FR**—Poisson-cocher grégaire

**LENGTH**  18 cm
**BIOLOGY**  Lives on outer reef slopes. Sometimes feeds in large groups on plankton in open water in front of an outer reef slope. Prefers areas with rising deepwater currents that are rich in plankton; 5–210 m.
**DISTRIBUTION**  Red Sea to Hawaii

ANGELFISHES—POMACANTHIDAE
Visible from far away because of their vivid poster colours, the larger angelfishes in particular move almost majestically across the reef. They are territorial: large *Pomacanthus* species have a territory of more than 1,000 m², while the smaller *Centropyge* species patrol an area of only a few square metres.
**CHANGING CLOTHES** The young of the Indo-Pacific *Pomacanthus* species all look very similar – dark blue to almost black, with white stripes. However, when they mature they undergo a dramatic colour change, and when this is complete the 'Emperor's new clothes' are completely different from the juvenile form.
**CHANGING SEX** Angelfishes mature sexually as females initially, but can subsequently change sex and become males (protogynous hermaphrodites). In most species, there is no difference in colour between the sexes, although an exception is the *Genicanthus* genus, in which males and females can sometimes differ quite markedly in their colouring.

## 1 | **Arabian angelfish** *Pomacanthus maculosus* —Angelfishes Pomacanthidae

**GER**—Arabischer Kaiserfisch  |  **FR**—Poisson-ange géographe

**LENGTH** 50 cm
**BIOLOGY** Individually but also sometimes in pairs. Relatively bold. This is one of the largest species. Its food includes sponges, leather corals and algae; 2–60 m.
**DISTRIBUTION** Red Sea, Arabian peninsula to Seychelles

## 2 | **Emperor angelfish** *Pomacanthus imperator* —Angelfishes Pomacanthidae

**GER**—Imperator-Kaiserfisch  |  **FR**—Poisson-ange impérial

**LENGTH** 40 cm
**BIOLOGY** Prefers coral-rich deep lagoons, coastal reefs and outer reef slopes. Has a large home territory. Mostly individually or in pairs, occasionally also in a harem. Feeds on sponges, sea squirts, cnidarians and algae; 3–80 m.
**DISTRIBUTION** Red Sea to French Polynesia

1

2

## 1 Regal angelfish *Pygoplites diacanthus*
—Angelfishes Pomacanthidae

**GER**—Pfauen-Kaiserfisch  |  **FR**—Poisson-ange duc

**LENGTH**  25 cm
**BIOLOGY**  Individually or in pairs; relatively common but shy: when approached, it retreats swiftly into crevices, near which it spends most of its time. Feeds on sponges and sea squirts; 1–80 m.
**DISTRIBUTION**  Red Sea to French Polynesia

## 2 Blue-girdled angelfish *Pomacanthus narvachus*
—Angelfishes Pomacanthidae

**GER**—Traum-Kaiserfisch  |  **FR**—Poisson-ange amiral

**LENGTH**  28 cm
**BIOLOGY**  Mostly individually, often close to its hiding place, relatively timid. Feeds principally on sponges and sea squirts. Rarely seen except in Indonesia; 3–30 m.
**DISTRIBUTION**  Indonesia to the Philippines and New Guinea

## 3 Bluering angelfish *Pomacanthus annularis*
—Angelfishes Pomacanthidae

**GER**—Ring-Kaiserfisch  |  **FR**—Poisson-ange à anneau

**LENGTH**  45 cm
**BIOLOGY**  Prefers coastal reefs with moderate growth of coral or rocky areas, often in turbid water. Adults frequently in pairs, otherwise solitary. Prefers areas close to cavities and in wrecks. Eats sponges and sea squirts; 5–45 m.
**DISTRIBUTION**  East Africa to south-west Japan, the Philippines and Solomon Islands

# Angelfishes

**1** | **Yellowface angelfish** *Pomacanthus xanthometopon*
—Angelfishes Pomacanthidae

**GER**—Gelbmasken-Kaiserfisch  |  **FR**—Poisson-ange à front jaune

**LENGTH** 38 cm
**BIOLOGY** Inhabits coral-rich lagoons and outer reef slopes. Usually solitary, sometimes also in pairs. Eats sponges and sea squirts; 5–15 m.
**DISTRIBUTION** Maldives to south-west Japan, western Micronesia, Great Barrier Reef and Vanuatu

**2** | **Threespot angelfish** *Apolemichthys trimaculatus*
—Angelfishes Pomacanthidae

**GER**—Dreipunkt-Kaiserfisch  |  **FR**—Poisson-ange à trois taches

**LENGTH** 25 cm
**BIOLOGY** Frequently on steep, coral-rich reef slopes; individually or in pairs, relatively timid. Feeds primarily on sponges and sea squirts. Juveniles live below 25 m and are well concealed; 3–40 m.
**DISTRIBUTION** East Africa, Maldives to Samoa

**3** | **Zebra lyretail angelfish** *Genicanthus caudovittatus*
—Angelfishes Pomacanthidae

**GER**—Rotmeer-Lyrakaiser  |  **FR**—Poisson-ange zébré de l'Océan Indien

**LENGTH** 20 cm
**BIOLOGY** Usually in harem groups consisting of a male and between five and nine females. Feeds mainly on zooplankton. Exhibits sexual dichromatism: males with zebra stripes, females plain pale grey; 15–70 m (usually below 25 m).
**DISTRIBUTION** Red Sea to Maldives

# Damselfishes

DAMSELFISHES—POMACENTRIDAE

**MINOR ROLE-PLAYERS** Damselfishes liven things up with their numerous species and large numbers, together with their bustling, lively behaviour. Reefs would be a great deal poorer without damselfishes. Yet, despite their importance within the reef community, they often receive little attention from divers, who consider damselfishes to be merely the bit players on the stage of the coral reef.

**STICKY EGGS** This successful family contains more than 320 species and lives mainly in tropical waters. Their food is often plankton or algae, but some species are omnivorous. Most species remain quite small at less than 10 cm in length: the Indo-Pacific sergeant, which can reach 20 cm, is considered one of the largest members of the family. This species is ideal for divers to observe the typical breeding behaviour of the damselfishes. First, a spot is chosen on a firm area of ground, and is then scrupulously cleaned. More than a thousand sticky eggs (depending on species) are laid on this spot. The clutch of eggs is then guarded until the fish hatch out, and oxygen-rich water is fanned over them.

## 1 | Golden damselfish *Amblyglyphidodon aureus*
—Damselfishes Pomacentridae

**GER**—Goldener Riffbarsch  I  **FR**—Demoiselle doré

**LENGTH** 14 cm
**BIOLOGY** Catches zooplankton in open water; prefers to live on outer reef slopes; 3–45 m.
**DISTRIBUTION** Andaman Sea, Cocos Islands to Fiji

## 2 | Indo-Pacific sergeant *Abudefduf vaigiensis*
—Damselfishes Pomacentridae

**GER**—Indopazifik-Sergeant  I  **FR**—Sergent-major de Mer Rouge

**LENGTH** 20 cm
**BIOLOGY** In shoals, preferably on outer edges of the reef, where it feeds on plankton; 0.5–15 m.
**DISTRIBUTION** Red Sea to French Polynesia

## 3 | Green chromis *Chromis viridis*
—Damselfishes Pomacentridae

**GER**—Blaugrüner Chromis  I  **FR**—Demoiselle bleue

**LENGTH** 9 cm
**BIOLOGY** In small shoals on *Acropora* branch coral, into which it retreats swiftly when threatened; 0.5–12 m.
**DISTRIBUTION** Red Sea to French Polynesia

ANEMONE FISHES—POMACENTRIDAE

**BED OF NETTLES** Without their anemone hosts these fishes would be easy prey for their many predators. Anemone fishes live close together among the stinging cells of the tentacles, and also snuggle down there for the night. They acquire an immunity to the stings when they are young by initially touching the tentacles very cautiously, though other animals suffer stings. Anemone fish fiercely defend their anemone against fish who might want to eat the tentacles, and exhibit defensive behaviour even towards divers perceived as threats.

**GIRL POWER** The largest and socially dominant fish in an anemone is always a female, and her immediate subordinate a male. These two form a permanent pair bond. Any other anemone fish living alongside this pair are invariably non-breeding juveniles. If the female dies, the highest-ranking male undergoes a sex change within a week and becomes the dominant female.

**1** | **False clown anemone fish** *Amphiprion ocellaris*
—Anemone fishes Pomacentridae

**GER**—Orange-Ringel-Anemonenfisch | **FR**—Poisson-clown à trois bandes

**LENGTH** 9 cm
**BIOLOGY** Lagoons and sheltered outer reef slopes. Often in small groups on one anemone. Present on three host anemones, including the magnificent anemone (*Heteractis magnifica*) as shown in the photo; 1–15 m.
**DISTRIBUTION** Andaman Sea to the Philippines and north-west Australia

**2** | **Clark's anemone fish** *Amphiprion clarkii*
—Anemone fishes Pomacentridae

**GER**—Clarks Anemonenfisch | **FR**—Poisson-clown de Clark

**LENGTH** 14 cm
**BIOLOGY** A variety of colour variants, mostly black with varying amounts of orange in the head area. The most widely distributed of all the anemone fish. Present on all 10 species of host anemone; 1–55 m.
**DISTRIBUTION** Arabian Gulf, Maldives to south Japan and Fiji

1
2

# Anemone Fishes

**1** | **Maldives anemone fish** *Amphiprion nigripes*
—Anemone fishes Pomacentridae

**GER**—Malediven-Anemonenfisch  I  **FR**—Poisson-clown des Maledives

**LENGTH** 11 cm
**BIOLOGY** Small area of distribution; lives exclusively on the magnificent anemone (*Heteractis magnifica*); 1–25 m.
**DISTRIBUTION** Maldives, Sri Lanka

**2** | **Pink anemone fish** *Amphiprion perideraion*
—Anemone fishes Pomacentridae

**GER**—Halsband-Anemonenfisch  I  **FR**—Poisson-clown à collier

**LENGTH** 10 cm
**BIOLOGY** Lives on the magnificent anemone, occasionally associates with up to three alternative host species; 3–30 m.
**DISTRIBUTION** South-east Thailand, Malaysia and Cocos Islands to Samoa

**3** | **Cinnamon clownfish** *Amphiprion melanopus*
—Anemone fishes Pomacentrida

**GER**—Schwarzflossen-Anemonenfisch  I  **FR**—Poisson-clown totré

**LENGTH** 12 cm
**BIOLOGY** Frequently in large colonies, lives on three different anemone species; 1–18 m.
**DISTRIBUTION** Sulawesi and Maluku Islands to French Polynesia

# Anemone Fishes

**1** | **Saddle anemone fish** *Amphiprion ephippium*
—Anemone fishes Pomacentridae

**GER**—Glühkohlen-Anemonenfisch  I  **FR**—Poisson-clown à selle

**LENGTH**  12 cm
**BIOLOGY**  Inhabits sheltered coastal reefs and bays. Very frequent in the Bubble-tip anemone, also in the Leathery sea anemone; 2–15 m.
**DISTRIBUTION**  Andaman Sea, West Malaysia, Sumatra and Java

**2** | **Yellow clownfish** *Amphiprion sandaracinos*
—Anemone fishes Pomacentridae

**GER**—Oranger Anemonenfisch  I  **FR**—Poisson-clown doré

**LENGTH**  13 cm
**BIOLOGY**  In lagoons and outer reefs, inhabits two species of anemone, usually in Merten's carpet sea anemone, less often in the Leathery sea anemone; 3–20 m.
**DISTRIBUTION**  Sumatra to north-west Australia, south-west Japan, the Philippines and Solomon Islands

**3** | **Spinecheek anemone fish** *Premnas biaculeatus*
—Anemone fishes Pomacentridae

**GER**—Stachel-Anemonenfisch  I  **FR**—Poisson-clown à joues épineuses

**LENGTH**  11 cm, rarely up to 16 cm
**BIOLOGY**  Lives exclusively on a single anemone species (*Entacmaea quadricolor*); 1–16 m.
**DISTRIBUTION**  Western Indonesia to Great Barrier Reef and Vanuatu

1
2
3

## WRASSES—LABRIDAE

This family is made up of about 500 species and has a characteristic swimming motion: forward movement is achieved using the pectoral fins only, and the tail fin is used only for high-speed swimming – when escaping, for example. These fish are active by day, often vividly coloured, and most of the smaller species are also agile swimmers. At night, the smaller species usually bury themselves in the sand, while the larger fish normally find a sheltered spot to rest in.

**NEW CLOTHES** All wrasses are thought to be sequential hermaphrodites: mature females are able to change into males later in life. In many species, different ages and genders can be distinguished by colour.

**CLEANING TEAM** Cleaner wrasses maintain cleaning stations where parasites and loose skin flakes are removed from the bodies of other fish. During this process the 'clients' usually remain still in the water, letting the cleaners into their mouths and between their gills. This skin hygiene makes an important contribution to the health of the client fish and provides the cleaners with their food.

### 1 | Humphead wrasse *Cheilinus undulatus* —Wrasses Labridae

**GER**—Napoleon I **FR**—Napoléon

**LENGTH** 230 cm

**BIOLOGY** The largest of the wrasses, weighing up to 190 kg. Timid by nature but in many areas has become accustomed to divers. Not common anywhere, it is solitary and has a large territory. It eats loricate invertebrates such as snails, molluscs and sea urchins. Heavily depleted in some areas because of its popularity in South-east Asian restaurants; 1–60 m.

**DISTRIBUTION** Red Sea to French Polynesia

### 2 | Broomtail wrasse *Cheilinus lunulatus* —Wrasses Labridae

**GER**—Besenschwanz-Lippfisch I **FR**—Vieille balayette

**LENGTH** 50 cm

**BIOLOGY** Usually solitary, on coral-rich reef edges with sand and gravel areas. Feeds mainly on bottom-dwelling invertebrates such as crustaceans, snails and molluscs. Spawns during the afternoon at high tide along the edges of the reef: one male lives with a harem of several females; 0.5–30 m.

**DISTRIBUTION** Red Sea to Arabian Gulf

**1** | **Bandcheek wrasse** *Oxycheilinus diagrammus*
—Wrasses Labridae

**GER**—Wangenstreifen-Lippfisch  |  **FR**—Vieille barbe noire

**LENGTH** 35 cm
**BIOLOGY** In coral-rich lagoons and outer reef slopes; often swims long distances across the seabed. A predator on small fish. Relatively bold, sometimes can even be curious; 2–60 m.
**DISTRIBUTION** Red Sea to Samoa

**2** | **Sixbar wrasse** *Thalassoma hardwicke*
—Wrasses Labridae

**GER**—Sechsstreifen-Junker  |  **FR**—Girelle taches d'encre

**LENGTH** 20 cm
**BIOLOGY** Shallow, coral-rich lagoons and outer reef slopes with clear water; frequently up on the reef top. Feeds on invertebrates and small fish from the seabed and open water; 1–15 m.
**DISTRIBUTION** East Africa to Polynesia

**3** | **Checkerboard wrasse** *Halichoeres hortulanus*
—Wrasses Labridae

**GER**—Schachbrett-Junker  |  **FR**—Lalo damier

**LENGTH** 27 cm
**BIOLOGY** An agile species in constant movement during the day. Frequent in clear lagoons and outer reef slopes. Feeds on bottom-dwelling invertebrates. The male exhibits territorial behaviour with extensive range; 1–30 m.
**DISTRIBUTION** Red Sea to French Polynesia

1
2
3

**1** | **Slingjaw wrasse** *Epibulus insidiator*
—Wrasses Labridae

**GER**—Stülpmaul-Lippfisch  I  **FR**—Épibule gourami

**LENGTH** 35 cm
**BIOLOGY** Coral-rich outer reef slopes; solitary and relatively timid. Eats shrimps, crustaceans and fish. Several colour variants but female typically exhibits uniform yellow colouration; 1–30 m.
**DISTRIBUTION** Red Sea to Polynesia

**2** | **Lyretail hogfish** *Bodianus anthioides*
—Wrasses Labridae

**GER**—Herzog-Lippfisch  I  **FR**—Labre à queue de lyre

**LENGTH** 21 cm
**BIOLOGY** In deep lagoons, bays and on its own in outer reef slopes. Solitary. The differently coloured juveniles often stay close to gorgonians, soft corals and bushy black corals for protection; 5–60 m. The older animals often swim over areas of sand and gravel in the reef, looking for bottom-dwelling invertebrates.
**DISTRIBUTION** Red Sea and East Africa to south Japan, Line Islands and French Polynesia

**3** | **Queen coris** *Coris formosa*
—Wrasses Labridae

**GER**—Königs-Junker  I  **FR**—Girelle reine

**LENGTH** 60 cm
**BIOLOGY** In coral-rich, usually exposed reefs. Males with vertical stripes, (photo: female). Swims alone over mixed zones of sand, corals and pebbles. Eats hard-shelled bottom-dwelling invertebrates; 3–30 m.
**DISTRIBUTION** Southern Red Sea and East Africa to Seychelles, Chagos, Maldives and Sri Lanka

PARROTFISHES—SCARIDAE

**STONE BITERS** Parrotfishes are attractive to look at – and can often also be heard. They use their beak-like mouths to scrape minute algae from rocks and coral, causing a scratching sound that can be heard over a considerable distance. They also scrape at living coral to obtain the symbiotic algae in the top layers of the skeleton. Some will bite off entire branches from branch corals, grinding them between their millstone-like pharyngeal teeth.

**MANY COLOURS** Parrotfishes can change sex from female to male during their lives, when they also change colour. Older males can have very vivid colouring; juveniles, too, often have a distinctive colour.

**SLEEPING BAG** Parrotfishes are frequently seen during night dives, asleep under ledges or wedged into crevices. Some species also cover themselves with a transparent cocoon of mucus, which acts as a scent barrier and protects them from nocturnal predators like moray eels, which detect their prey by scent.

---

**1** | **Humphead parrotfish** *Bolbometapon muricatum* —Parrotfishes Scaridae

GER—Büffelkopf-Papageifisch   I   **FR**—Perroquet bossu vert

**LENGTH** 130 cm
**BIOLOGY** The largest species of the family, grows up to weigh at least 70 kg. Feeds on living coral, from which it bites off entire branches. Also eats algae. Sleeps at night in a group inside large crevices and caves. Cautious and locally uncommon in most areas; 1–50 m.
**DISTRIBUTION** Red Sea to French Polynesia

---

**2** | **Roundhead parrotfish** *Scarus strongylocephalus* —Parrotfishes Scaridae

GER—Indischer Buckelkopf   I   **FR**—Perroquet à tête arrondie

**LENGTH** 70 cm
**BIOLOGY** Common, widespread and relatively large species. Swims alone or in pairs in lagoons and on outer reef slopes. Adults are also very rarely seen patrolling in shoals. Females have reddish undersides and yellow-green backs; 2–35 m.
**DISTRIBUTION** Gulf of Aden to south-west Indonesia

1

2

# Parrotfishes

**1** | **Blue-barred parrotfish** *Scarus ghobban*
—Parrotfishes Scaridae

**GER**—Blauband-Papageifisch  |  **FR**—Perroquet barbe bleue

**LENGTH** 75 cm
**BIOLOGY** Usually in sheltered rocky and coral reefs with sandy and pebbly substrate, often with more turbid water. Juveniles also in groups above seagrass meadows. Males blue-green (photo: female); 5–35 m.
**DISTRIBUTION** Red Sea and East Africa to south-west Japan, Galápagos, Panama and French Polynesia

**2** | **Rusty parrotfish** *Scarus ferrugineus*
—Parrotfishes Scaridae

**GER**—Rostnacken-Papageifisch  |  **FR**—Perroquet rouille

**LENGTH** 40 cm
**BIOLOGY** Males (**2a**) are blue with green markings; females (**2b**) are brownish with a yellow tail. Common, relatively bold. Male is territorial and has a harem consisting of several females. Covers itself with a slimy cocoon at night; 1–60 m.
**DISTRIBUTION** Red Sea to Arabian Gulf

**1** | **Bullethead parrotfish** *Chlororus sordidus*
— Parrotfishes Scaridae

**GER**—Kugelkopf-Papageifisch   I   **FR**—Perroquet marguerite

**LENGTH** 40 cm
**BIOLOGY** A very common species, relatively bold. Lives in lagoons, on reef tops and outer reef slopes; juveniles frequently on seaweed and gravel. Can sometimes travel long distances during the day between its feeding and sleeping places; 1–30 m.
**DISTRIBUTION** Red Sea to Polynesia

**2** | **Longnose parrotfish** *Hipposcarus harid*
— Parrotfishes Scaridae

**GER**—Indische Langnase   I   **FR**—Perroquet chevalin

**LENGTH** 75 cm
**BIOLOGY** Deep lagoons, coves and semi-sheltered outer reef slopes. Often on sand and gravel, where it grazes on blanket weed. Frequently seen in small groups consisting of a male and several harem females; 1–30 m.
**DISTRIBUTION** Red Sea to Java

**3** | **Bicolour parrotfish** *Cetoscarus bicolor*
— Parrotfishes Scaridae

**GER**—Masken-Papageifisch   I   **FR**—Perroquet ronille

**LENGTH** 80 cm
**BIOLOGY** The juveniles (see photograph) of this species have very distinctive colouring. They mostly swim across small sandy areas between blocks of coral, and are frequently seen by divers; 1–30 m.
**DISTRIBUTION** Red Sea to French Polynesia

## SANDPERCH—PINGUIPEDIDAE

This predator typically lies in wait supported on its ventral fins and with its head raised slightly to give it a better view, usually on sandy areas but in some cases also on gravel, rock or coral. They dart quickly forwards to catch invertebrates and small fish. The males are territorial, and have a harem of several females.

### 1 | Speckled sandperch *Parapercis hexophthalma*
—Sandperch Pinguipedidae

**GER**—Schwanzfleck-Sandbarsch  |  **FR**—Pinge pintade

**LENGTH**  28 cm
**BIOLOGY**  Male and female sandperch can often be distinguished by slight variations in their colour pattern. This is also true of this species: the male has bands on its cheeks, while the female has dots. Feeds on bottom-dwelling invertebrates. Sleeps under gravel at night. The male has a harem of two to five females; spawning takes place at sunset; 2–22 m.
**DISTRIBUTION**  Red Sea to Fiji

## SAND-DIVERS—TRICHONOTIDAE

These very elongated fish are sequential hermaphrodites: the females are able to change into males in later life. The male is identified by the thread-like spines on its dorsal fin, which it raises when mating, together with its pectoral fins. Males are territorial and have a harem. Feed on zooplankton.

### 2 | Red Sea sand-diver *Trichonotus nikii*
—Sand-divers Trichonotidae

**GER**—Rotmeer-Sandtaucher  |  **FR**—Anguille de sable

**LENGTH**  12 cm
**BIOLOGY**  Lives on sheltered sandy slopes in coves. Usually in a small group close to the bottom – not more than 1–3 m above it – and feeds on zooplankton. When threatened it dives instantly head-first into the sand, where it also spends the night; 2–90 m.
**DISTRIBUTION**  Red Sea. There are very similar species in other Indo-Pacific regions

**TUNA AND MACKEREL—SCOMBRIDAE**
Tuna are perfectly designed for speed: a spindle-shaped body that is rigid at the front and has a narrow tailstock and a tall, curved tail fin. They are the real pacemakers of the ocean, reaching top speeds of up to 95 kph. Untiring swimmers, they cover long distances in their search for food, and eat up to a quarter of their bodyweight every day.

**1** | **Dogtooth tuna** *Gymnosarda unicolor*
—Tuna and Mackerel Scombridae

**GER**—Einfarben-Thunfisch  |  **FR**—Thon dents de chien

**LENGTH**  220 cm
**BIOLOGY**  White mouth opening with large fangs. Swims alone or in small groups, patrolling open water along deep lagoons, channels and outer reef slopes. This high-speed predator hunts in particular for fusiliers and other plankton-feeders. Relatively bold, occasionally inquisitive when approached by divers; 1–100 m.
**DISTRIBUTION**  Red Sea to French Polynesia

**TRIPLEFINS—TRIPTERYGIIDAE**
Triplefins get their name from their three dorsal fins. It is the only family on the coral reef that has this distinctive feature, but it is usually difficult to identify because the fins are very close together. These tiny, elongated bottom-dwellers feed on small invertebrates of the seabed. Often overlooked, not just because of their small size but because many are very well camouflaged.

**2** | **Striped triplefin** *Helcogramma striata*
—Triplefins Tripterygiidae

**GER**—Gestreifter Dreiflosser  |  **FR**—Triptérygion strié

**LENGTH**  4 cm
**BIOLOGY**  This is one of the very few species that are eye-catching and attractively coloured. It is also common, and is often seen by divers. These fish rest on corals, sponges and other hard surfaces. They are found individually or in small groups, and are tolerant of close human approach when unthreatened; 0.5–15 m.
**DISTRIBUTION**  Indonesia to Line Islands; there is a similar species in the Maldives

1

2

# Blennies

**BLENNIES—BLENNIIDAE**
The 350 species in this family have no scales, or only very small, smooth ones; instead, they have a protective mucous coating.
**SEDENTARY**  Blennies live on hard ground and have a small burrow. They lay their eggs on the ground – in cracks, under stones, or in empty shells. The brood is often guarded by the male, and sometimes by both parents. The males have small territories, which they defend against their rivals. There are two species that live in coral reefs: combtooth blennies have small, comb-like teeth for scraping tiny blanket-weed algae from hard surfaces and eating small invertebrates. The Midas blenny eats zooplankton. Sabretooth blennies are predators with long, curved eyeteeth, and are usually active swimmers. Some specialist species bite scales, skin mucus and even pieces of fin from larger fish.
**WOLF IN SHEEP'S CLOTHING**  To do this, some sabretooth blennies mimic harmless species. The false cleanerfish mimics genuine cleaner wrasses (see p. 116) in its colouring and swimming motion in order to get close to its victims.

## 1 | Red Sea mimic blenny *Escenius gravieri*
—Blennies Blenniidae

**GER**—Mimikry-Kammzähner  |  **FR**—Blennie imitatrice de la mer Rouge

**LENGTH**  8 cm
**BIOLOGY**  Mimics the poisonous Blackline fangblenny to protect itself from predators; 2–20 m.
**DISTRIBUTION**  Red Sea to Gulf of Aden

## 2 | Midas blenny *Escenius midas*
—Blennies Blenniidae

**GER**—Neonaugen-Kammzähner  |  **FR**—Blennie Midas

**LENGTH**  13 cm
**BIOLOGY**  There are bluish-grey and yellow variants, the latter mimicking the Scalefin anthias (see p. 66) and mingling with their shoals; 2–35 m.
**DISTRIBUTION**  Red Sea to Polynesia

## 3 | Bluestriped blenny *Plagiotremus rhinorhynchus*
—Blennies Blenniidae

**GER**—Blaustreifen-Säbelzähner  |  **FR**—Blennie à bandes bleues

**LENGTH**  12 cm
**BIOLOGY**  Bites off scales and pieces of fin from other fish. Juveniles mimic young cleaner wrasses; 1–40 m.
**DISTRIBUTION**  Red Sea to French Polynesia

# Dragonets



DRAGONETS—CALLIONYMIDAE

There are about 125 species of dragonet, making them a relatively large family, but they often go unnoticed. Most species remain very small, well below 10 cm. In addition, all dragonets are bottom-dwelling species that remain on sandy or muddy seabeds – not the diver's preferred environment. Finally, many species are able to burrow in the sand, and often do so during the day. If this were not enough, most species have the same colouring as their backgrounds, so they are well camouflaged. It would be quite possible to omit them here were it not for a few species that are spectacularly coloured and are particular favourites of photographers in many diving areas. Virtually no one wants to miss the courtship dance of the mandarin fish, one of the most popular photographic 'models'. In most dragonet species the males are more brightly coloured; mating is preceded by a lengthy courtship ritual.

## 1 | Mandarin fish *Synchiropus splendidus*
—Dragonets Callionymidae

**GER**—Mandarinfisch  |  **FR**—Poisson-mandarin

**LENGTH**  6 cm
**BIOLOGY**  Common in some areas, but hides on soft ground with thick gravel, or in coral branches. Is also present in more turbid water. They mate at sunset, when pairs swim straight up from the seabed with their bodies in close contact; 3–30 m.
**DISTRIBUTION**  Indonesia, south Japan, the Philippines to New Guinea

## 2 | Fingered dragonet *Dactylopus dactylopus*
—Dragonets Callionymidae

**GER**—Finger-Leierfisch  |  **FR**—Dragonnet dactylé

**LENGTH**  18 cm
**BIOLOGY**  Lives on sheltered sand or gravel ground close to a reef or near the shore. Often buried during the day; raises its dorsal fins if disturbed. Feeds on small bottom-dwelling invertebrates; 1–55 m.
**DISTRIBUTION**  Tropical western Pacific e.g. the Philippines, Indonesia, Papua New Guinea

1

2

**GOBIES—GOBIIDAE**
**A BIG FAMILY** With more than 2,000 species, gobies are the largest family of marine fish. Most of them are small, bottom-dwelling fish without a swim bladder. Some species change sex, others do not. Many live in holes, sometimes alone and sometimes in those occupied by other creatures.
**WATCHDOGS AND BUILDERS** Some species live in a close symbiotic relationship with the snapping rock-boring shrimp. This shrimp is almost blind and digs a burrow in the sand up to 50 cm long, sometimes with more than one entrance. The goby eats minute invertebrates, including those exposed by the shrimp's digging and maintenance activities. In return for receiving shelter on a sandy seabed that otherwise provides no cover, the fish's role in the partnership is that of a watchdog. When the shrimp wishes to deposit a load of sand in the open, it always keeps one antenna in contact with the goby, which retreats deep into the burrow at the slightest disturbance, accompanied by the shrimp. A note of interest: a goby of the Maldives (*Trimmaton natans*), only 8 mm long, is the smallest vertebrate on earth.

## 1 | Gold-headed sleeper goby *Valenciennea strigata* —Gobies Gobiidae

**GER**—Goldstirn-Schläfergrundel  I  **FR**—Gobie akahachihaze

**LENGTH**  18 cm
**BIOLOGY**  Juveniles in groups, adults mainly in pairs and close together; 1–20 m.
**DISTRIBUTION**  Southern Red Sea to French Polynesia

## 2 | Citron goby *Gobiodon citrinus* —Gobies Gobiidae

**GER**—Zitronen-Korallengrundel  I  **FR**—Gobie corail citron

**LENGTH**  6.5 cm
**BIOLOGY**  Sits in branched coral, individually or in groups. It is covered with a bitter and possibly poisonous skin mucus (protection against predators); 1–25 m.
**DISTRIBUTION**  Red Sea to Samoa

## 3 | Signal goby *Signigobius biocellatus* —Gobies Gobiidae

**GER**—Krabbenaugen-Grundel  I  **FR**—Gobie à deux ocelles

**LENGTH**  6.5 cm
**BIOLOGY**  Lives in sheltered reefs. Its 'eyes' are to frighten predators by giving the impression of great size; 1–30 m.
**DISTRIBUTION**  Indonesia and the Philippines to Solomon Islands and Great Barrier Reef

# Gobies

**1** | **Orange-dash goby** *Valenciennea puellaris*
—Gobies Gobiidae

**GER**—Maiden-Schläfergrundel  |  **FR**—Gobie à tirets orange

**LENGTH**  14 cm
**BIOLOGY**  Builds a burrow under lumps of gravel, removing the sand with its mouth. Usually in pairs at burrow entrance; darts instantly into the burrow when threatened; feeds on small invertebrates; 2–30 m.
**DISTRIBUTION**  Red Sea to Samoa

**2** | **Aurora goby** *Amblyeleotris aurora*
—Gobies Gobiidae

**GER**—Aurora-Wächtergrundel  |  **FR**—Gobie symbiotique magnifique

**LENGTH**  9 cm
**BIOLOGY**  Lives on coarse coral sand, on reef tops and shallow outreef areas. Lives in symbiosis with the snapping shrimp, *Alpheus randalli;* 1–35 m.
**DISTRIBUTION**  East Africa to Maldives and Andaman Sea

**3** | **Whipcoral goby** *Bryaninops yongei*
—Gobies Gobiidae

**GER**—Peitschenkorallen-Zwerggrundel  |  **FR**—Gobie de corail-fouet

**LENGTH**  3 cm
**BIOLOGY**  Lives exclusively on whip coral – two fish often live on a single coral, which they do not leave. If disturbed, they dart round to the other side; 3–45 m.
**DISTRIBUTION**  Red Sea to Polynesia

1
2
3

**JAWFISHES—OPISTOGNATHIDAE**
Jawfishes have a massive head with very large eyes and mouth, but they feed on zooplankton. They use their powerful jaws to build almost vertical burrows in sand or gravel, strengthening them from the inside with small stones and fragments of coral and shell. Their homes resemble a brick-lined well, giving them the popular name of 'well-diggers'. All species are mouth breeders.

**1** | **Gold-specs jawfish** *Opistognathus randalli*
—Jawfishes Opistognathidae

**GER**—Randalls-Brunnenbauer | **FR**—Poisson-puits de Randall

**LENGTH** 11 cm
**BIOLOGY** Typically observed protruding from its burrow entrance. After mating, the male takes the fertilized eggs in his mouth. The ball, containing hundreds of eggs, is well protected there and is supplied with fresh, oxygen-rich water. The young hatch after about five days, when they have to fend for themselves; 3–20 m.
**DISTRIBUTION** Indonesia to the Philippines

**DARTFISHES—PTERELEOTRIDAE**
Dartfishes, sometimes referred to as torpedo or arrow gobies, are small, elongated fish that live on sand, gravel, scree or muddy sediment. Typically they live in pairs; some also live in small or large groups. They never move far from their shelters, into which they rush when threatened. They feed on zooplankton, which they catch from passing currents while hovering above the ground.

**2** | **Fire dartfish** *Nemateleotris magnifica*
—Dartfishes Ptereleotridae

**GER**—Feuer-Schwertgrundel | **FR**—Poisson de feu

**LENGTH** 7 cm
**BIOLOGY** Relatively common on hard ground, often in pairs but also singly or in groups; hovers close to the ground, darts into its burrow when threatened; 6–60 m.
**DISTRIBUTION** East Africa to Hawaii and Pitcairn Islands

**SPADEFISHES — EPHIPPIDAE**
A favourite of divers and photographers, spadefishes are large, handsome and not at all timid – indeed, they can be curious and will swim around divers, especially in popular diving spots. In addition, they usually appear in photogenic groupings, sometimes even in large shoals. It is not unusual to see them at cleaner stations. They can change the brightness of their colour very quickly from silvery white to a dark smoky colour.
**FALLING LEAVES** The bodies of spadefishes are flattened laterally and are disc-shaped. Their mouths are small in relation to their overall size, and they have small, brush-like teeth. Juveniles vary considerably in terms of colour and body shape. They have very elongated dorsal, anal and ventral fins, which become smaller as they grow older. The young of some species turn over sideways when threatened so that they look like leaves floating in the current.

**1** | **Longfin spadefish** *Platax teira*
— Spadefishes Ephippidae

**GER**—Langflossen-Fledermausfisch  I  **FR**—Platax à longues nageoires

**LENGTH** 60 cm
**BIOLOGY** Individually or in schools, on a reef slope or in front of it in open water. Juveniles stay close to the reef, preferring shallow, sheltered places; 1–20 m.
**DISTRIBUTION** Red Sea to Fiji

**2** | **Circular spadefish** *Platax orbicularis*
— Spadefishes Ephippidae

**GER**—Rundkopf-Fledermausfisch  I  **FR**—Poule d'eau

**LENGTH** 57 cm
**BIOLOGY** Individually or in schools, frequently along steep slopes. Juveniles are pelagic and sometimes enter coves in sheltered places such as a landing stage. Their colour and movements give them the appearance of dead leaves; 2–34 m.
**DISTRIBUTION** Red Sea to French Polynesia

1

2

**RABBITFISHES—SIGANIDAE**
**SOCIABLE** Rabbitfishes move around in pairs or groups, sometimes in shoals of several hundred. About half of the roughly 30 species live in schools when young, but form pairs later. The other species remain in schools all their lives.
**DISCREET SLEEPERS** Rabbitfishes rest at night, lying down sideways on the seabed without seeking shelter. They have the ability to change colour very quickly, and camouflage themselves when sleeping, when they become a less distinct colour with marbling and flecks.
**NIBBLERS** It is rare to see rabbitfishes at rest: they spend most of their time in a ceaseless search for food. They feed mainly on algae and seaweed, and also on invertebrates such as sea squirts and sponges. When feeding, the small mouth with its thicker top lip makes characteristic nibbling movements, which is what gives them their name.
**CAUTION** Unlikely as it seems, these inoffensive creatures have numerous venomous spines, which they use for defence and can cause painful injuries.

## 1 | Two-barred rabbitfish *Siganus virgatus*
— Rabbitfishes Siganidae

**GER**—Zweiband-Kaninchenfisch  |  **FR**—Sigan à deux bandes

**LENGTH** 33 cm
**BIOLOGY** Usually swims in pairs in shallow coastal waters; occasionally ventures into fresh water; 2–25 m.
**DISTRIBUTION** Southern India to West Papua

## 2 | Gold-spotted rabbitfish *Siganus stellatus laqueus*
— Rabbitfishes Siganidae

**GER**—Tüpfel-Kaninchenfisch  |  **FR**—Sigan tacheté doré

**LENGTH** 40 cm
**BIOLOGY** Common and relatively bold. Adults in pairs, juveniles in groups. Patrols a large territory, feeds on blanket weed; 1–40 m.
**DISTRIBUTION** Red Sea, Gulf of Aden

## 3 | Golden rabbitfish *Siganus guttatus*
— Rabbitfishes Siganidae

**GER**—Indischer Kaninchenfisch  |  **FR**—Sigan raies d'or

**LENGTH** 43 cm
**BIOLOGY** Juveniles frequently among seaweed, adults form small schools on coastal reefs; 2–15 m.
**DISTRIBUTION** Andaman Sea to West Papua

SURGEONFISHES—ACANTHURIDAE
This family is divided into scalpel, unicorn and saw surgeonfishes. Most of the first group graze minute blanketweed algae from rocks. Others, especially the Naso species, feed on zooplankton. Like other algae-feeders, the grazing surgeonfishes play an important role in the ecological balance of the reef. An experiment was carried out in which nets were used to keep algae-feeding fish away from particular parts of a reef. Within a very short time, these areas experienced an explosive growth of blanket weed that overran the coral and had a serious negative impact.
**STILETTOS**  The sharp blades of bone on each side of the tailstock are what gives the family its name. Scalpel surgeonfish have a blade on each side, which fits into a groove. When they turn their tails sideways, the blade on the outer curve of the tail jumps out like a switchblade. Unicorn and saw surgeonfishes, however, have fixed blades.

## 1 | Powderblue surgeonfish *Acanthurus leucosternon*
—Surgeonfishes Acanthuridae

**GER**—Weißkehl-Doktorfisch  I  **FR**—Poisson-chirurgien à poitrine blanche

**LENGTH**  23 cm
**BIOLOGY**  Lives on clearwater outreef tops; singly, sometimes also in large groups; 1–25 m.
**DISTRIBUTION**  East Africa to west Indonesia

## 2 | Yellowmask surgeonfish *Acanthurus mata*
—Surgeonfishes Acanthuridae

**GER**—Grauer Doktorfisch  I  **FR**—Chirurgien à masque jaune

**LENGTH**  50 cm
**BIOLOGY**  Frequently found in groups at the edge of a reef. Changes colour at cleaner stations; 5–45 m.
**DISTRIBUTION**  Red Sea to French Polynesia

## 3 | Sohal surgeonfish *Acanthurus sohal*
—Surgeonfishes Acanthuridae

**GER**—Arabischer Doktorfisch  I  **FR**—Chirurgien zébré

**LENGTH**  40 cm
**BIOLOGY**  Frequently seen at the edge of the reef top, likes to be in the 3-m zone. The male defends a small feeding territory; 0.3–10 m.
**DISTRIBUTION**  Red Sea to Arabian Gulf

## 1 | Convict surgeonfish *Acanthurus triostegus*
—Surgeonfishes Acanthuridae

**GER**—Sträflings-Doktorfisch  |  **FR**—Chirurgien bagnard

**LENGTH** 27 cm
**BIOLOGY** Usually travels the reef in a large group and can sometimes invade the territory of other algae feeders despite its relatively small size; 1–90 m.
**DISTRIBUTION** East Africa to Panama

## 2 | Lined surgeonfish *Acanthurus lineatus*
—Surgeonfishes Acanthuridae

**GER**—Blaustreifen-Doktorfisch  |  **FR**—Chirurgien rayé

**LENGTH** 38 cm
**BIOLOGY** Frequently in the surf zone of outer reef tops and exposed reef edges. Very territorial, large males have feeding territories and harems which they defend aggressively. Grazes on algae; 0.2–6 m.
**DISTRIBUTION** East Africa to south-west Japan, Micronesia and French Polynesia

## 3 | Blackspot surgeonfish *Acanthurus bariene*
—Surgeonfishes Acanthuridae

**GER**—Rammkopf-Doktorfisch  |  **FR**—Chirurgien à ocelle

**LENGTH** 42 cm
**BIOLOGY** In coastal and outer reefs with clear water. The bulging forehead becomes enlarged with age. Roams singly or in small groups over the reef and grazes on algal film; 6–50 m.
**DISTRIBUTION** East Africa to south-west Japan, Palau, Solomon Islands and Great Barrier Reef

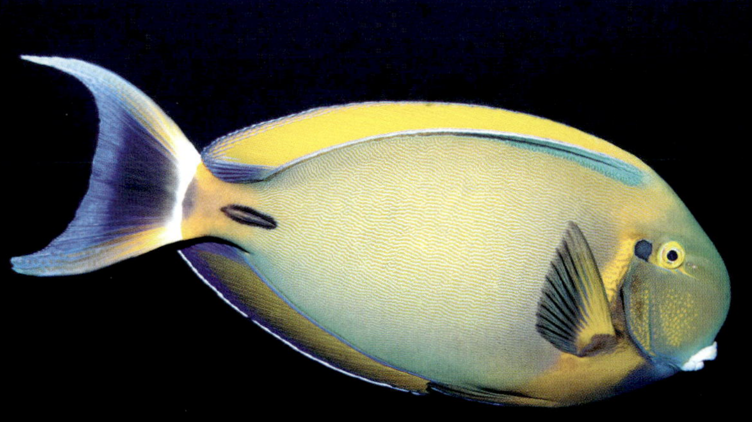

# Surgeonfishes

**1** | **Palette surgeonfish** *Paracanthurus hepatus*
—Surgeonfishes Acanthuridae

**GER**—Paletten-Doktorfisch  |  **FR**—Chirurgien palette

**LENGTH**  26 cm
**BIOLOGY**  Prefers clear outer reefs with a good current. Swims in small, loose groups 1–3 m above the ocean floor and eats zooplankton. Juveniles often stay in the protection of branched corals; 2–40 m.
**DISTRIBUTION**  East Africa to south-west Japan, Line Islands and Samoa

**2** | **Yellowtail tang** *Zebrasoma xanthurum*
—Surgeonfishes Acanthuridae

**GER**—Blauer Segelflosser  |  **FR**—Acanthure à queue jaune

**LENGTH**  22 cm
**BIOLOGY**  Inhabits coral-rich reefs with channels and caves. Individually or in small groups. Grazes on blanket weed on dead coral, gravel and rocks; 0.5–22 m.
**DISTRIBUTION**  Red Sea to Arabian Gulf and Sri Lanka

**3** | **Sleek unicornfish** *Naso hexacanthus*
—Surgeonfishes Acanthuridae

**GER**—Blauschwanz-Nasendoktor  |  **FR**—Nason lisse

**LENGTH**  75 cm
**BIOLOGY**  A common species, usually in groups, tends not to move more than a few metres away from the reef. Feeds on large zooplankton. Able to change colour rapidly; 6–137 m.
**DISTRIBUTION**  Red Sea to south-west Japan, Hawaii, Micronesia, French Polynesia and Pitcairn Islands

1
2
3

# Surgeonfishes

## 1 | Bignose unicornfish *Naso vlamingi*
—Surgeonfishes Acanthuridae

**GER**—Masken-Nasendoktor  I  **FR**—Nason à gros nez

**LENGTH**  75 cm
**BIOLOGY**  Usually swims in loose groups high on the reef, hunting for large zooplankton. Changes colour dramatically and quickly at cleaner stations and during mating; 4–50 m.
**DISTRIBUTION**  East Africa to French Polynesia

## 2 | Elegant unicornfish *Naso elegans*
—Surgeonfishes Acanthuridae

**GER**—Indischer Gelbklingen-Nasendoktor  I  **FR**—Nason à éperons orange

**LENGTH**  45 cm
**BIOLOGY**  In lagoons and outer reefs, relatively common. Sometimes in small loose groups. Grazes on algae from dead corals, and rocky and pebbly substrates. Large males occasionally lay claim to a territory. Spawns in pairs; 1–90 m.
**DISTRIBUTION**  Red Sea and East Africa to south Oman, Andaman Sea and Bali

## 3 | Spotted unicornfish *Naso brevirostris*
—Surgeonfishes Acanthuridae

**GER**—Schärpen-Nasendoktor  I  **FR**—Nason tacheté

**LENGTH**  60 cm
**BIOLOGY**  In deep lagoons and along outer reef slopes. Mostly in small groups in open water beyond the reef where it eats zooplankton. In contrast, juveniles and sub-adults graze on algal film. This species can rapidly change its colouring from dark brown to pale whitish; 1–50 m.
**DISTRIBUTION**  Red Sea and East Africa to south-west Japan, Hawaii and Ducie Island

1

2

3

## MOORISH IDOL — ZANCLIDAE

When glimpsed briefly, this fish could pass as a *Heniochus* (see p. 100). However, it is not related to this species but to the surgeonfish. Apart from that it is the sole representative of its family, which consists of only one species: the Moorish idol.

**1** | **Moorish idol** *Zanclus cornutus*
— Moorish idol Zanclidae

**GER**—Halfterfisch  |  **FR**—Tranchoir

**LENGTH**  22 cm
**BIOLOGY**  Lives on reefs of rock and coral, moves above the reef in pairs or small groups, occasionally in large schools. Feeds mainly on sponges but also on other animal and plant life. Its pelagic larval stage is very long, so it has a very wide range of distribution. It does not go to live down on the reef until it is almost fully grown; 1–145 m.
**DISTRIBUTION**  East Africa, Maldives to Mexico

## BARRACUDAS — SPHYRAENIDAE

Barracudas are powerful, active predators. They can accelerate very quickly – more quickly than any other marine fish – and catch their prey with a rapid forward lunge. With its powerful jaws and sharp teeth, a barracuda can easily bite in half a fish as big as itself.

**2** | **Great barracuda** *Sphyraena barracuda*
— Barracudas Sphyraenidae

**GER**—Großer Barrakuda  |  **FR**—Grand barracuda

**LENGTH**  190 cm
**BIOLOGY**  Juveniles often in groups, adults usually solitary. Often remains motionless in open water beside or above the reef. Curious, may approach divers, but generally not dangerous unless provoked; 1–198 m.
**DISTRIBUTION**  Red Sea to Polynesia and tropical Atlantic

1

2

**TRIGGERFISHES—BALISTIDAE**
Triggerfishes prepare shallow sandy pits where they lay their eggs. The eggs are defended against predators, and even against divers in some larger species. In this situation the diver should move away from the nest immediately. Apart from during the breeding season, even the largest species are placid.
**CRUNCHY** Triggerfishes have powerful jaws with chisel-shaped teeth, which they use to crack open even hard-shelled species such as molluscs, snails, coral, sea urchins and crustaceans. They often use a jet of water to expose prey hidden under the sand; it is mainly the larger species that use this method.
**ANCHORED** When threatened, triggerfishes escape into crevices in the reef – they do this also to rest at night. They raise the first spine on their dorsal fin to wedge themselves in. The lower part of the second spine pushes into an indentation at its base, holding the first spine in an upright position. The fish is now securely anchored in its hiding place, and a predator would have great difficulty in pulling it out.

## 1 | Picasso triggerfish *Rhinecanthus assasi*
—Triggerfishes Balistidae

**GER**—Arabischer Picassodrücker  I  **FR**—Baliste picasso arabe

**LENGTH**  30 cm
**BIOLOGY**  Solitary and territorial, usually close to a hiding place. Fairly timid; 1–25 m.
**DISTRIBUTION**  Red Sea to Arabian Gulf

## 2 | Orange-lined triggerfish *Balistapus undulatus*
—Triggerfishes Balistidae

**GER**—Orangestreifen-Drückerfisch  I  **FR**—Baliste ondulé

**LENGTH**  30 cm
**BIOLOGY**  Makes a shallow nest pit in sand or gravel when spawning. Individually or in small groups; 1–50 m.
**DISTRIBUTION**  Red Sea to French Polynesia

## 3 | Redtoothed triggerfish *Odonus niger*
—Triggerfishes Balistidae

**GER**—Rotzahn-Drückerfisch  I  **FR**—Baliste dents rouges

**LENGTH**  40 cm
**BIOLOGY**  Outer reef slopes with strong currents, frequently in large groups in open water, catching zooplankton; 3–55 m.
**DISTRIBUTION**  Red Sea to French Polynesia

**1** | **Titan triggerfish** *Balistoides viridescens*
—Triggerfishes Balistidae

**GER**—Riesen-Drückerfisch  |  **FR**—Baliste olivâtre

**LENGTH**  75 cm
**BIOLOGY**  Largest species, usually solitary, relatively bold. In pairs while caring for the eggs, which it lays in a hollow in the sand. Caution: will attack divers who get too close to the eggs; 1–40 m.
**DISTRIBUTION**  Red Sea to French Polynesia

**2** | **Yellow-spotted triggerfish** *Pseudobalistes fuscus*
—Triggerfishes Balistidae

**GER**—Blaustreifen-Drückerfisch  |  **FR**—Baliste jaune et bleu

**LENGTH**  55 cm
**BIOLOGY**  Can occasionally be seen blowing sand away with a jet of water to expose prey; 0.5–50 m.
**DISTRIBUTION**  Red Sea to French Polynesia

**3** | **Yellow-margin triggerfish** *Pseudobalistes flavimarginatus*
—Triggerfishes Balistidae

**GER**—Gelbsaum-Drückerfisch  |  **FR**—Baliste face jaune

**LENGTH**  60 cm
**BIOLOGY**  Often in lagoons and in coves with seaweed. Feeds on coral and bottom-dwelling invertebrates, which it exposes by blowing a jet of water. May be aggressive while guarding eggs; 2–50 m.
**DISTRIBUTION**  Red Sea to French Polynesia

1
2
3

### 1 | Clown triggerfish *Balistoides conspicillum*
—Triggerfishes Balistidae

**GER**—Leoparden-Drückerfisch  I  **FR**—Baliste clown

**LENGTH** 50 cm
**BIOLOGY** Timid and solitary, with a large territory; clear, coral-rich outer reef slopes; juveniles are a different colour and live mainly below 20 m in areas with plenty of hiding places; 1–75 m.
**DISTRIBUTION** East Africa to Samoa

### 2 | Pinktail triggerfish *Melichthys vidua*
—Triggerfishes Balistidae

**GER**—Witwen-Drückerfisch  I  **FR**—Baliste veuf

**LENGTH** 35 cm
**BIOLOGY** Inhabits clear outer reef slopes. Swims singly or in loose groups up to a few metres above the substrate; 4–60 m.
**DISTRIBUTION** East Africa to south Japan, Hawaii, Galápagos and French Polynesia

### 3 | Gilded triggerfish *Xanthichthys auromarginatus*
—Triggerfishes Balistidae

**GER**—Blaukehl-Drückerfisch  I  **FR**—Baliste à liseré d'or

**LENGTH** 22 cm
**BIOLOGY** Prefers outer reef slopes. Often swims in loose shoals a few metres above the reef and hunts zooplankton in the open water; 15–150 m.
**DISTRIBUTION** Mauritius to south-west Japan, Micronesia, Hawaii and French Polynesia

## FILEFISHES—MONACANTHIDAE

Filefishes swim slowly and sedately, can manoeuvre skilfully, and often hover motionless on the spot. Most of the smaller species live in concealment or camouflaged, and prefer to stay close to cover, to which they often have a similar colouring – seaweed, horn coral or soft coral. Most filefishes live individually or in pairs, sometimes also in small groups, and eat a variety of foods, including algae, seaweed, sponges, worms and crustaceans. Some species, however, are genuine specialist feeders.

**ROUGH SKIN** Filefishes are close relatives of the triggerfish, and like them have an extended primary dorsal fin spine that can be raised and folded back. They have a tough, leathery skin with very small scales carrying minute spikes, and they feel rough like sandpaper – hence the name 'filefish'. The non-poisonous Blacksaddle filefish mimics the venomous Valentin's sharpnose puffer, which it very closely resembles.

**1** | **Scrawled filefish** *Aluterus scriptus*
—Filefishes Monacanthidae

**GER**—Schrift-Feilenfisch  |  **FR**—Bourse écriture

**LENGTH** 100 cm
**BIOLOGY** Solitary and not often seen. Juveniles live in the open sea (pelagic) in the shelter of jellyfish or seaweed; 2–80 m.
**DISTRIBUTION** Circumtropical

**2** | **Harlequin filefish** *Oxymonacanthus halli*
—Filefishes Monacanthidae

**GER**—Rotmeer-Palettenstachler  |  **FR**—Bourse arlequin

**LENGTH** 7 cm
**BIOLOGY** Feeds exclusively on Acropora staghorn coral; a very similar species is distributed from East Africa to Samoa; 0.3–30 m.
**DISTRIBUTION** Red Sea

**3** | **Blacksaddle filefish** *Paraluteres prionurus*
—Filefishes Monacanthidae

**GER**—Schwarzsattel-Feilenfisch  |  **FR**—Fausse bourse

**LENGTH** 11 cm
**BIOLOGY** Singly or in small groups; mimics the venomous Valentin's sharpnose puffer (see p. 174); 1–25 m.
**DISTRIBUTION** Gulf of Aden, Maldives to Marshall Islands

BOXFISHES—OSTRACIIDAE

**MASTERS OF MANOEUVRE** Boxfishes are slow swimmers, but they make up for it with their manoeuvring skills. They use precision movements of their fins to turn round on the spot, rotate like a helicopter, and even swim backwards. Their precision swimming involves very little body movement – it is achieved instead by a complex interaction of their fins.

**IMMOBILE** They have no alternative, because more than three-quarters of their body length is covered by a rigid, immobile bony armour. The hard, angular external armour is made up of (mainly) hexagonal bony plates, and the honeycomb shape of the plates is readily visible in some species. As well as their armour, boxfishes have another defence against predators: they secrete a highly effective toxic mucus from skin glands. These protective and warning measures frighten off many potential predators.

**VARIED COLOURS** In many species males and females are different colours, and in some species the juveniles also (see photographs right).

**1** | **Yellow boxfish** *Ostracion cubicus*
—Boxfishes Ostraciidae

**GER**—Gelbbrauner Kofferfisch  |  **FR**—Coffre jaune

**LENGTH** 45 cm

**BIOLOGY** In lagoons and areas of outer reefs that are not too exposed, usually in coral-rich areas. Solitary. Relatively common, only moderately shy. Large males are blue-grey with a nasal bulge (**1a**), females (**1b**). The juveniles (**1c**) are a striking lemon-yellow with black spots and are found in protected areas, such as small overhangs, or between rocks or branched corals. Adults also swim over open areas. Feeds on various small invertebrates on the seabed, as well as on growth algae; 1–40 m.

**DISTRIBUTION** Red Sea and East Africa to south-west Japan, New Zealand and French Polynesia

1a
1b 
1c

# Boxfishes

**1** | **Solor boxfish** *Ostracion solorensis*
— Boxfishes Ostraciidae

**GER**—Solor-Kofferfisch  I  **FR**—Poisson-coffre à peau dure

**LENGTH**  11 cm
**BIOLOGY**  Timid, lives in hiding. Prefers coral-rich outer reef slopes. Males have a dark blue background, females (pictured) brown to green; 1–20 m.
**DISTRIBUTION**  Indonesia to the Philippines, Papua New Guinea and Great Barrier Reef

**2** | **Spotted boxfish** *Ostracion meleagris*
— Boxfishes Ostraciidae

**GER**—Weißpunkt-Kofferfisch  I  **FR**—Poisson-coffre pintade

**LENGTH**  16 cm
**BIOLOGY**  Solitary, prefers clear lagoons and outer reefs. Usually in protected areas. Feeds on various small invertebrates, sea squirts and sponges. Males (**2a**) develop from females (**2b**) through sexual reversal; 1–40 m.
**DISTRIBUTION**  East Africa to South Japan, Hawaii, Galápagos, Mexico, Australia and French Polynesia

**1** | **Reticulate boxfish** *Ostracion rhinorhynchos*
—Boxfishes Ostraciidae

**GER**—Großnasen-Kofferfisch  I  **FR**—Poisson à nageoires rayonnées

**LENGTH**  35 cm
**BIOLOGY**  Inhabits pebbly and sandy areas close to coral in deep lagoons and sheltered areas in outer reefs. Generally rare in most areas. Feeds on small, bottom-dwelling invertebrates; 3–40 m.
**DISTRIBUTION**  East Africa to south Japan, Palau and Australia

**2** | **Longhorn cowfish** *Lactoria cornuta*
—Boxfishes Ostraciidae

**GER**—Langhorn-Kofferfisch  I  **FR**—Poisson-vache à longues cornes

**LENGTH**  46 cm
**BIOLOGY**  Has two pairs of 'horns' on head and rear body. Fairly rare, solitary; on sand, gravel and seaweed meadows. Feeds on bottom-dwelling invertebrates, which it can expose by blowing a jet of water; 1–100 m.
**DISTRIBUTION**  Red Sea to Polynesia

**3** | **Thornback cowfish** *Lactoria fornasini*
—Boxfishes Ostraciidae

**GER**—Rückendorn-Kofferfisch  I  **FR**—Poisson-vache à épine dorsale

**LENGTH**  15 cm
**BIOLOGY**  Prefers clear lagoons and outer reef slopes; swims close to the seabed, on seaweed meadows, sand and gravel surfaces; male is highly territorial; 1–30 m.
**DISTRIBUTION**  East Africa to South Japan, Hawaii and French Polynesia

1
2 
3

**PUFFERFISHES—TETRAODONTIDAE**

Pufferfishes are ponderous swimmers but can manoeuvre themselves with great skill, turn round on the spot or swim backwards. They eat many different plant and animal species; their powerful, beak-like mouths can crack open even hard-shelled prey. They can blow themselves up like a balloon by taking in water; this frightens predators, and makes the puffer too big to fit into the predator's mouth. They also have a bitter taste.

**A DEADLY BALL** The primary defence of pufferfishes is neurotoxic defence via tetrodotoxin – one of the deadliest poisons in nature. It causes paralysis of the muscles, including the breathing muscles, which can lead to asphyxiation. Even sharks will spit out unharmed a pufferfish they have caught if they taste that their prey is poisonous. In certain specialized restaurants in Japan, licensed fugu chefs prepare the pufferfish so that it causes only minor, deliberate poisoning. Elsewhere, however, preparing the fish without proper knowledge has led to many fatal cases of poisoning.

## 1 | Map puffer *Arothron mappa*
—Pufferfishes Tetraodontidae

**GER**—Mappa-Kugelfisch  |  **FR**—Poisson-ballon griffonné

**LENGTH** 60 cm

**BIOLOGY** The map puffer has an unmistakable 'maze' pattern that radiates out from its eyes. It is a solitary species but relatively bold. Can be seen both in lagoons and on outer reef slopes. It feeds on sponges, sea squirts, snails and algae; 4–40 m.

**DISTRIBUTION** East Africa, Maldives to Samoa

## 2 | Star puffer *Arothron stellatus*
—Pufferfishes Tetraodontidae

**GER**—Riesen-Kugelfisch  |  **FR**—Poisson-ballon étoilé

**LENGTH** 100 cm

**BIOLOGY** The largest species in the family. The star puffer is seen relatively frequently; it is solitary and feeds on sea urchins, starfish, crustaceans, coral, algae etc. It likes to rest on a sandy seabed, but it is also not unusual to see it several metres away from the reef, swimming at a leisurely pace through open water; 2–52 m.

**DISTRIBUTION** Red Sea to French Polynesia

1

2

**1** | **Masked puffer** *Arothron diadematus*
—Pufferfishes Tetraodontidae

**GER**—Masken-Kugelfisch | **FR**—Poisson-globe masqué

**LENGTH** 30 cm
**BIOLOGY** This solitary species is Red Sea endemic and frequently
encountered. It often rests on the seabed, and can also be seen on night
dives. During the breeding season it often moves around in fairly large
groups; 3–25 m.
**DISTRIBUTION** Red Sea

**2** | **Black-spotted puffer** *Arothron nigropunctatus*
—Pufferfishes Tetraodontidae

**GER**—Schwarzflecken-Kugelfisch | **FR**—Poisson-ballon à taches noires

**LENGTH** 30 cm
**BIOLOGY** Cream, grey, blue-grey, green-grey, brownish, sometimes
yellow, but always with black spots. Feeds on coral, sea squirts and
sponges; 1–35 m.
**DISTRIBUTION** East Africa, Maldives to Line and Cook Islands

**3** | **White-spotted puffer** *Arothron hispidus*
—Pufferfishes Tetraodontidae

**GER**—Weißflecken-Kugelfisch | **FR**—Poisson-ballon à taches blanches

**LENGTH** 50 cm
**BIOLOGY** Found in lagoons, bays and outer reefs with mixed substrate of
corals, sand and pebbles, also on seagrass meadows. Common species,
often found resting on the bottom. Eats sponges, sea squirts, crustaceans,
corals, starfish, mussels and algae; 1–50 m.
**DISTRIBUTION** Red Sea and East Africa to south Japan, Hawaii, Panama
and French Polynesia

## 1 | **Narrow-lined puffer** *Arothron manilensis*
—Pufferfishes Tetraodontidae

**GER**—Streifen-Kugelfisch  I  **FR**—Poisson-ballon pyjama

**LENGTH** 31 cm
**BIOLOGY** In lagoons, bays and sheltered outer reefs. Occupies seagrass meadows and sandy areas close to reefs; 1–20 m.
**DISTRIBUTION** Borneo and Bali to the Philippines, south-west Japan, Micronesia, Samoa and eastern Australia

## 2 | **Valentin's sharpnose puffer** *Canthigaster valentini*
—Pufferfishes Tetraodontidae

**GER**—Sattel-Spitzkopfkugelfisch  I  **FR**—Canthigaster à selles

**LENGTH** 10 cm
**BIOLOGY** Males have a territory with up to seven females, all of which lay their eggs in bush algae. Eggs contain tetrodotoxin; larval emergence occurs within 3–5 days; 1–55 m.
**DISTRIBUTION** Gulf of Aden, Maldives to French Polynesia

## 3 | **Papuan toby** *Canthigaster papua*
—Pufferfishes Tetraodontidae

**GER**—Flecken-Spitzkopfkugelfisch  I  **FR**—Canthigaster papou

**LENGTH** 10 cm
**BIOLOGY** Coral-rich lagoons and outer reefs. Feeds on thread and crusting algae, coral and invertebrates; 1–36 m.
**DISTRIBUTION** Indonesia, Papua New Guinea to Palau. Very similar species *C. solandri* from East Africa, Maldives to Polynesia

**PORCUPINEFISHES — DIODONTIDAE**
**SHARK V. PORCUPINEFISH** A battle with a predictable outcome? Perhaps. But this juicy morsel has stuck in the throat of many a predator. When threatened, porcupinefishes swallow water and blow themselves up like a balloon so they are up to four times their normal size. They then get stuck in the predator's throat. Even large sharks and groupers can choke on a porcupinefish. Do not handle these docile fish to induce them to 'blow up' as the stress and the handling may be life-threatening to the fish.
**A SPIKED MACE** The spines of porcupinefishes make them easy to distinguish from the very similar pufferfishes. Some porcupinefishes have fixed spines, others can raise and lower them. When blown up and with their spines sticking out, these 'spiked maces' are an impregnable stronghold for most predators.
**NOCTURNAL BITERS** Like the pufferfish, their closest relative, porcupinefishes have a beak-shaped mouth. It can bite with great force and crack open hard-shelled prey such as molluscs, snails, sea urchins or hermit crabs. Porcupinefishes have strikingly large eyes and tend to be nocturnal. During the day, most of them rest in caves or crevices, or underneath ledges.

## 1 | **Balloonfish** *Diodon liturosus*
—Porcupinefishes Diodontidae

**GER**—Masken-Igelfisch  |  **FR**—Poisson porc-épic à épines courtes

**LENGTH** 50 cm
**BIOLOGY** Rests in cracks or under ledges during the day, feeds at night on hard-shelled invertebrates; 5–90 m.
**DISTRIBUTION** Red Sea to French Polynesia

## 2 | **Spot-fin porcupinefish** *Diodon hystrix*
—Porcupinefishes Diodontidae

**GER**—Gepunkteter Igelfisch  |  **FR**—Poisson porc-épic tacheté

**LENGTH** 80 cm
**BIOLOGY** Rests during the day, usually under ledges or in caves, less frequently swimming in open sea near the reef; 2–50 m.
**DISTRIBUTION** Circumtropical

## 3 | **Orbicular burrfish** *Cyclichthys orbicularis*
—Porcupinefishes Diodontidae

**GER**—Kurzstachel-Igelfisch  |  **FR**—Poisson porc-épic bécard

**LENGTH** 15 cm
**BIOLOGY** In sheltered reefs, hides during the day. Hunts at night for prawns, molluscs and worms; 2–20 m.
**DISTRIBUTION** Red Sea to south Japan and north Australia

—Reptiles &
Marine Mammals

## SEA TURTLES—CHELONIIDAE AND DERMOCHELYIDAE

Sea turtles are able to cover vast distances across the oceans, and have been shown to travel more than 11,000 km. Like migratory birds, they use the earth's magnetic field to guide them. Mating takes place at sea, and the females crawl on to land to lay their eggs, usually returning to their own place of birth.

**1** | **Green sea turtle** *Chelonia mydas*
— Sea turtles Cheloniidae

**GER**—Grüne Schildkröte  |  **FR**—Tortue verte

**LENGTH** 153 cm
**BIOLOGY** Comes to land roughly every two to three years to lay its eggs. The incubation period usually lasts between 45 and 60 days. The sex of the offspring is determined by the temperature of the nest: above 30 °C only females develop, below 30 °C mainly males. Sea turtles (seven species) feed on seaweed, jellyfish, sponges and soft coral, among other food sources. They have to come up to the surface to breathe.
**DISTRIBUTION** All tropical and subtropical seas

## SEA SNAKES—ELAPIDAE

Sea snakes were formerly land-dwellers and have lungs, so they have to come up to the surface to breathe. Even so, they are excellent divers, some diving down as far as 100 m, although most stay in shallower waters. They can often be seen in cracks and crevices on the reef, busily searching for small prey, mainly fish.

**2** | **Black & white sea krait** *Laticauda colubrina*
— Sea snakes Elapidae

**GER**—Gelblippen-Seekobra  |  **FR**—Tricot rayé à lèvres jaunes

**LENGTH** 150 cm (larger in Fiji)
**BIOLOGY** This is the species most often seen by divers in its distribution area. It belongs to the small group of flat-tail sea snakes, which – unlike most other species – go on land to rest, mate and lay their eggs. Feeds mainly on moray eels. Venomous but behaviourally non-confrontational.
**DISTRIBUTION** Sri Lanka and eastern India to Tonga

1
2

**DUGONG—DUGONG DUGON**
Their name says it all: 'sea cows' graze on seaweed meadows. This method of nutrition makes the dugong unique: it is the world's only plant-eating mammal that lives exclusively in the sea. Its close relatives, the manatees, from the south-eastern United States, all live in fresh water.

**1** | **Dugong** *Dugong dugon*
—Dugong Dugongidae

**GER**—Dugong | **FR**—Dugong

**LENGTH** Up to 350 cm
**BIOLOGY** Lives in wide, shallow coves with seagrass meadows. Grows to at least 400 kg and up to a maximum of 900 kg, and can live for 70 years. A single calf is born after a gestation period of 13–15 months, and a strong and very close bond is formed between mother and calf. The young dugong feeds from its mother for up to 18 months.
**DISTRIBUTION** Red Sea to Vanuatu, but nowadays only sporadically

**DOLPHINS—DELPHINIDAE**
Dolphins are highly developed, intelligent and social marine mammals. Their streamlined shape makes them fast, skilled swimmers and good divers. They navigate and find their prey using echolocation, and they communicate by means of complex acoustic signalling.

**2** | **Indo-Pacific bottlenose dolphin** *Tursiops aduncus*
—Dolphins Delphinidae

**GER**—Kleiner Tümmler | **FR**—Grand dauphin de l'océan Indien

**LENGTH** 260 cm
**BIOLOGY** Biologists are still uncertain whether the greater and lesser bottlenose dolphins are two different species or just sub-species. The lesser bottlenose, however, lives mainly in coastal waters, and tends to stay within its 300 km$^2$ territory. Present on many reefs in the Red Sea and the Maldives, it is a regular sight.
**DISTRIBUTION** Red Sea to Australia and Japan

1

2

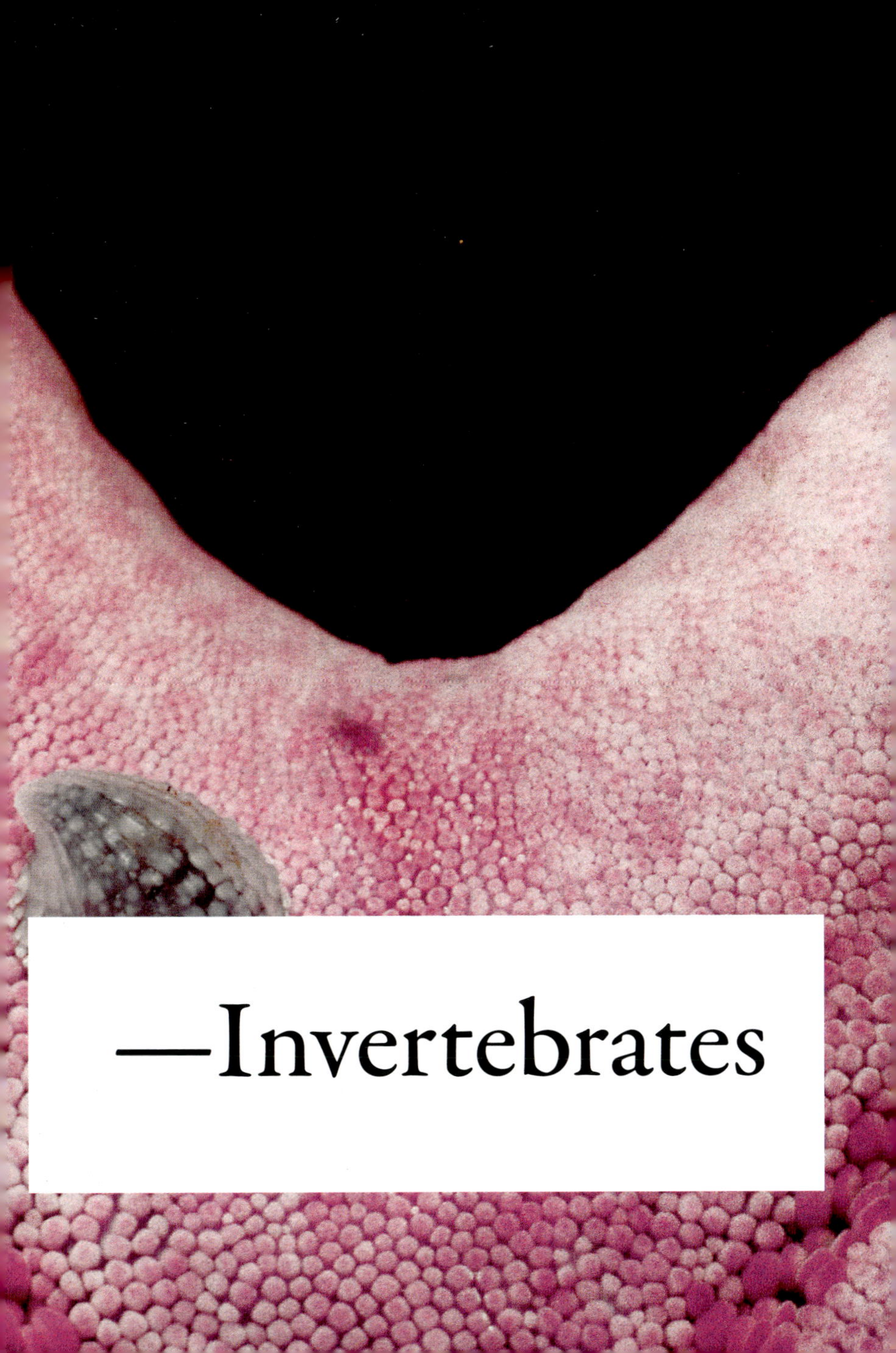

—Invertebrates

# Sponges



**PUMPING STATION** Around 8,000 species of sponge have already been recorded, but marine biologists are constantly discovering new ones, and estimate that there are about 25,000 species in total. Sponges feed on minute particles by taking in the water around them through tiny pores on their surface, pumping it through a network of channels and retaining the food particles, and then pumping out the filtered water through large outlet openings. A sponge the size of a football can process about 3,000 litres of water every day, filtering out up to 99 per cent of the bacteria, single-celled algae and organic particles held in it.

**PHARMACY ON THE SEABED** Sponges possess a huge variety of chemical antigens that protect them from predators and prevent them from becoming overgrown. This chemical arsenal is a goldmine for pharmaceutical researchers because some of these substances can be used in medicine. A number of drugs have already been developed from sponges, including treatments for viral infections and cancer.

## 1 | Red Sea sponge *Negombata corticata* —Sponges Podospongiidae

**GER**—Pracht-Geweihschwamm  |  **FR**—Éponge rouge de la mer Rouge

**LENGTH** 70 cm

**BIOLOGY** Branched like fingers or antlers. At the slightest injury or pressure, this species exudes a red liquid, which is highly toxic to fish and causes the fish to move away immediately. The sponge is eaten mainly by the Pyjama nudibranch (see p. 220), which uses the toxin from the sponge (latrunculin) for its own defence.

**DISTRIBUTION** Red Sea, Indian Ocean

## 2 | Barrel sponge *Xestospongia testudinaria* —Sponges Petrosiidae

**GER**—Tonnenschwamm  |  **FR**—Éponge baril

**LENGTH** 150 cm, diameter up to 50 cm

**BIOLOGY** Varies from barrel- to vase-shaped. On the outside it has deep, irregular vertical corrugations that increase the surface area for the countless minute inlet openings. The largest tropical sponge, it frequently hosts commensal macrofauna including feather stars, small sea cucumbers (*Synaptula* spp.) or the pink hairy squat (*Lauriea siagiani*).

**DISTRIBUTION** Indonesia, New Guinea to the Philippines

1
2

**FIRE CORALS—MILLEPORIDAE**
Because of their sturdy limestone skeleton, fire corals are often thought to
be stone corals. In fact, like the sea ferns, they belong to the hydrozoa. Just
like reef-building stone corals they live in symbiosis with single-celled
algae, and form part of the reef structure with their limestone framework.
There are net, plate and encrusted species.

**1** | **Net fire coral** *Millepora dichotoma*
     | —Fire corals Milleporidae

**GER**—Netz-Feuerkoralle  |  **FR**—Corail de feu ramifié

**LENGTH** 60 cm
**BIOLOGY** Surface covered with minute holes, in each of which there is a
polyp (*Millepora* means 'thousand pores'). Because of its light-dependent
algae (zooxanthellae) it colonizes the higher parts of the reef. Widespread
in some areas on reef edges and well-lit slopes. Caution: nematocyst
discharge induces acute dermatological reaction, such as a burning
sensation, inflammation and welts.
**DISTRIBUTION** Red Sea to Samoa

**SEA FERNS—PLUMULARIIDAE**
Sea ferns are found in all oceans in a variety of species, some with
powerful stings. Typical growth forms are feather, bush and tree shapes.
Some are very delicate and lacy with few branches, others are much
sturdier and heavily branched. The colonies can range in size from a few
centimetres to species that are 1 m in height.

**2** | **Stinging hydroid** *Macrorhynchia philippina*
     | —Sea ferns Plumulariidae

**GER**—Philippinen-Farn  |  **FR**—Hydroïde piquant des Philippines

**LENGTH** 30 cm
**BIOLOGY** Colonizes hard ground, usually in places with a good current
flow. Probably migrated to the Mediterranean via the Suez Canal. The
colonies look delicate but in fact are very robust, and are anchored in
the ground by root-like runners. Can sting if touched, and may trigger an
allergic reaction.
**DISTRIBUTION** Worldwide in tropical seas

1

2

JELLYFISHES — SCYPHOZOA

Jellyfishes are present in every ocean, from the tropics to the Arctic, from the surface to the lowest depths. The approximately 200–250 species have an umbrella diameter ranging from a few centimetres to over 2 m.

**SETTLERS AND NOMADS** The life cycle of most species has an alternation of generations. The small polyp stage, which remains fixed on the seabed, changes into the freely swimming medusa stage, which roams across the oceans and with which we are familiar. The next generation is then the polyp stage, and the cycle begins once again.

**GLUTTON** Many species live only for a year, some only a few months. During this time they eat a lot. The common or moon jellyfish consumes up to 20,000 plankton every day, and larger species correspondingly more. In this way even the largest species grow to their full size in a matter of months.

**SLIMMING DIET** Many jellyfishes go through long periods of starvation when they lose huge amounts of weight. Animals with an umbrella diameter of 40 cm can shrink down to about 2.5cm in diameter. When sufficient food is available, they quickly grow back to their old size.

## 1 | Crown jellyfish *Cephea cephea* —Jellyfishes Cepheidae

**GER**—Blaue Wurzelmundqualle  |  **FR**—Méduse couronne

**LENGTH** 15 cm
**BIOLOGY** Pelagic species, also brought by currents close to the shore. Sting is very weak, often unnoticed.
**DISTRIBUTION** Red Sea to Polynesia

## 2 | Common or Moon jellyfish *Aurelia* sp. —Moon jellyfishes Ulmaridae

**GER**—Ohrenqualle  |  **FR**—Méduse Aurélie

**LENGTH** Maximum 50 cm
**BIOLOGY** Locally common, can form huge swarms. Most have very weak stings.
**DISTRIBUTION** Several species worldwide; *A. Maldivensis* (25 cm): Red Sea, Indian Ocean

## 3 | Upside-down jellyfish *Cassiopea andromeda* —True jellyfish Cassiopeidae

**GER**—Mangrovenqualle  |  **FR**—Méduse inversée

**LENGTH** 12 cm
**BIOLOGY** In shallow waters up to 15 m. Lies on its 'back' to give maximum sunlight to its zooxanthellae.
**DISTRIBUTION** Red Sea to western Pacific

1
2
3

**SOFT CORALS—ALCYONARIA**

**PINCUSHION** Soft corals have numerous limestone nodules embedded in their fleshy tissues. Most of these nodules are very small, but some can be up to 1 cm long, as in the *Dendronephthya* species. These species shrink when they lose water, when the nodules protrude clearly.

**CHEMICAL CUDGEL** In addition, soft corals contain many chemical antigens. Most species are highly toxic to fish, or are at the very least protected by the deterrent action of their anti-predator substances.

**ADAPTATION** Very few predators are immune to such chemical weapons. Some butterfly fish occasionally nibble off polyps of soft coral, while sea turtles can eat entire colonies. Some sea slugs, too, are specialist feeders on specific soft corals. Many species live in symbiosis with photosynthesizing zooxanthellae, whose products contribute substantially to the coral's nutrition. The brightly-coloured species have no symbiotic algae and feed on plankton.

## 1 | Klunzinger's soft coral *Dendronephthya klunzingeri*
—Soft corals Nephtheidae

**GER**—Klunzingers Bäumchenkorallel  |  **FR**—Corail mou de Klunzinger

**LENGTH** 100 cm

**BIOLOGY** Forms magnificent growths in some areas. Mostly pink to purplish-red; colour is not an indication of species, which can only be established with certainty from the nodules. Often shrinks during the day following water loss; in many areas exhibits nocturnal suspension feeding after diurnal contraction.

**DISTRIBUTION** Red Sea to western Pacific

## 2 | Vibrant soft coral *Dendronephthya hemprichi*
—Soft corals Nephtheidae

**GER**—Hemprichs Bäumchenkoralle  |  **FR**—Corail mou d'Hemprich

**LENGTH** 70 cm

**BIOLOGY** Tree-like, but branches are mostly in two dimensions only. Orange or pink. Only a few years ago it was discovered that this species feeds almost exclusively on minute plankton algae. The effectiveness of this plant food source is demonstrated by young specimens in particular, which can achieve growth rates of more than 8 per cent per day.

**DISTRIBUTION** Red Sea to western Pacific

1

2

**1** | **Lobate leather coral** *Lobophytum* sp.
—Leather corals Alcyoniidae

**GER**—Lappige Lederkoralle  I  **FR**—Corail cuir à doigt

**LENGTH** 70 cm (width)
**BIOLOGY** Nutrition augmented by the photosynthesis of zooxanthellae, so lives in well-lit places.
**DISTRIBUTION** Red Sea to western Pacific

**2** | **Common toadstool coral** *Sarcophyton trocheliophorum*
—Leather corals Alcyoniidae

**GER**—Pilz-Lederkoralle  I  **FR**—Corail cuir géant

**LENGTH** 80 cm (width)
**BIOLOGY** Relies on symbiotic zooxanthellae for enhanced nutrition via photosynthesis, and therefore lives in brightly lit environments.
**DISTRIBUTION** Red Sea to western Pacific

**3** | **Finger leather coral** *Sinularia leptoclados*
—Leather corals Alcyoniidae

**GER**—Kurzfinger-Lederkoralle  I  **FR**—Sinulaire à doigts courts

**LENGTH** 30 cm (per clump)
**BIOLOGY** Has densely-packed calcium sclerites, which form a dense adhesive mass at the base of the colony. Can form columns several metres high, thus forming part of the reef structure.
**DISTRIBUTION** Red Sea to western Pacific

1
2
3

# Horn Corals

## HORN CORALS—ALCYONACEA

Horn corals have a supporting skeleton that is firm but flexible, made up of limestone nodules bonded together, in most cases with a horn-like substance, gorgonin, which forms a fibrous bond. This flexible core is surrounded by a soft bark in which the polyps are embedded.

**MANY MOUTHS** The surface is densely covered with polyps – many thousands, in the case of large fan colonies. When open, they form a giant, fine-meshed net, which catches plankton carried in by the current. The polyps act like a single organism with many mouths. It is not essential for an individual polyp to feed, as long as the adjacent polyps do so, which then share the nutrition obtained.

In order to catch plankton more effectively, fan gorgonians grow at right angles to the current. All species that do not have zooxanthellae live by catching plankton, and are often vividly coloured. There are also species with zooxanthellae, which grow in shallow waters with good light and are more muted in colour.

**1** | **Knotted fan** *Melithaea ochracea*
—Sea fans Melithaeidae

**GER**—Knotenfächer  |  **FR**—Gorgone noueuse

**LENGTH** 100 cm
**BIOLOGY** Lives on steep reef slopes, catches microplankton. Colour variable but mainly pink, orange-red or purple.
**DISTRIBUTION** Indian Ocean, western Pacific

**2** | **Giant sea fan** *Annella mollis*
—Fan corals Subergorgiidae

**GER**—Riesen-Fächerkoralle  |  **FR**—Gorgone géante

**LENGTH** 200 cm
**BIOLOGY** Pale cream in the Red Sea, elsewhere yellowish, or orange-red. Prefers exposed, steep reef slopes.
**DISTRIBUTION** Red Sea to western Pacific

**3** | **Red cluster whip** *Ellisella juncea*
—Reed corals Ellisellidae

**GER**—Binsengorgonie  |  **FR**—Gorgone-balais orange

**LENGTH** 60 cm
**BIOLOGY** Likes an exposed position with a strong current. Like all colourful gorgonians, does not have zooxanthellae.
**DISTRIBUTION** Red Sea to western Pacific

1
2
3

**SEA FEATHERS—PENNATULACEA**

Sea feathers colonize sandy and muddy surfaces. They have a fleshy stem and a powerful burrowing foot, with which they anchor themselves deep in the soft ground. They generally stay in one location, but if necessary they can move away by alternately spreading and elongating the foot in order to find a better position.

## 1 | Common sea feather *Pteroides* sp.
—Sea feathers Pennatulacea

**GER**—Dunkle Seefeder  I  **FR**—Plume de mer

**LENGTH** up to 60 cm

**BIOLOGY** Sea feathers are nocturnal and catch zooplankton. During the day, they usually bury themselves completely in the sediment. The colony is able to contract and open out by expelling and taking in water respectively. Small commensal crustaceans often live among the polyps, where they find food and shelter.

**DISTRIBUTION** Red Sea to western Pacific

**CRUST ANEMONES—ZOANTHARIA**

Most species of crust anemone form colonies. The polyps measure barely 1 cm or 2 cm across, but they can build colonies of more than a thousand individuals, forming huge cushions that cover large areas. Some species (*Palythoa*) are known to contain the highly poisonous palytoxin.

## 2 | Button polyp *Palythoa* sp.
—Crust anemones Sphenopidae

**GER**—Schirmchen-Krustenanemone  I  **FR**—Polype bouton

**LENGTH** 1 cm (diameter of polyp)

**BIOLOGY** Crust anemones are very difficult to identify, so most of them are known only by their generic name. Many have a rough feel because they incorporate silicon-containing particles or grains of sand in their tissues. Many have symbiotic algae, and are brownish or greenish in colour accordingly.

**DISTRIBUTION** Indian and Pacific Oceans

1
2

## TUBE-DWELLING ANEMONES — CERIANTHARIA

The group contains about 50 species and lives on sandy ground in all seas, from shallow water to deep oceans. Tube-dwelling anemones have a worm-like foot with a pointed base for burrowing in the sand. They make a parchment-like tube from mucus and sand into which they retract when threatened. They use their tentacles to catch zooplankton.

### 1 | Giant tube anemone *Cerianthus* cf. *filiformis*
—Tube-dwelling anemones Cerianthidae

**GER**—Große Zylinderrose  |  **FR**—Anémone tube géante

**LENGTH**  30 cm
**BIOLOGY**  Like all species, it has short mouth tentacles, which push its prey into its throat, surrounded by long, sticky tentacles for catching. As in other species, the colour of the long tentacles varies, ranging in this case from white to brown, blue or purple, always with pale-coloured mouth tentacles. Catches mainly plankton at night, possibly also small fish.
**DISTRIBUTION**  In large areas of Indo-Pacific

## DISC ANEMONES — CORALLIMORPHARIA

Disc anemones are closely related to stone corals, and look like anemones without tentacles, but they have no skeleton. Some species live singly, others can form large carpets measuring several metres across. Worldwide there are roughly 50 species; some have strong stinging capsules and can give a painful sting.

### 2 | Balloon corallimorph *Amplexidiscus fenestrafer*
—Disc anemones Corallimorphidae

**GER**—Große Scheibenanemone  |  **FR**—Anémone oreille d'éléphant

**LENGTH**  45 cm
**BIOLOGY**  Lives on sheltered reefs, sometimes in groups, usually between 10 m and 30 m on gravel or dead coral. Its main source of food is the photosynthesis of its symbiotic zooxanthellae, but it also catches zooplankton and possibly small fish by slowly closing its large, doughnut-shaped disc into a ball. Can sting with a painful burn if touched.
**DISTRIBUTION**  Indo-Pacific

1

2

## SEA ANEMONES—ACTINIARIA

Sea anemones look like plants but are cnidarians, and are predatory feeders. They live individually but can also cluster together in dense groups. Most species have long, conspicuous tentacles that contain stinging capsules, but only a few of the roughly 1,000 species are able to give a noticeable sting to a human – and very few a powerful one.

Sea anemones live anchored to rocky or sediment ground, spending most of their lives in the same spot. However, if necessary, they are able to move slowly. If threatened, many species form a ball or withdraw quickly into crevices or into their mud burrows. They use their tentacles to catch minute organisms from the water, but can also eat crustaceans and fish.

**FELLOWSHIP** Many species host zooxanthellae, which provide almost all their nutritional needs. Some are home to various crustaceans and fish. Anemone fish in particular sometimes defend their host resolutely against predators.

## 1 | Magnificent anemone *Heteractis magnifica* —Carpet anemones Stichodactylidae

**GER**—Pracht-Anemone  |  **FR**—Anémone magnifique

**LENGTH** Diameter 100 cm
**BIOLOGY** Frequently a host for anemone fish, and also for damselfish, shrimps and porcelain crabs; stem usually vividly coloured, e.g. blue, purple, red, nut-brown or white. Has photosynthesizing zooxanthellae, which contribute to its nutrition; also catches zooplankton. Typically in exposed locations; 1–30 m.
**DISTRIBUTION** Red Sea to French Polynesia

## 2 | Adhesive anemone *Cryptodendron adhaesivum* —Partner anemones Thalassianthidae

**GER**—Noppenrand-Anemone  |  **FR**—Anémone adhésive

**LENGTH** Diameter 35 cm
**BIOLOGY** Colour variable: green, brown, olive, sometimes very colourful. The tentacles are small and very sticky. This species withdraws quickly into a rock crevice if disturbed. Rarely colonized by anemone fish (*A. clarkii*, if at all), but often by partner shrimps (*Periclimenes bevicarpalis*).
**DISTRIBUTION** Red Sea to western Pacific

1

2

# Stone Corals



STONE CORALS—SCLERACTINIA

**MASTER BUILDERS** Stone corals are a vital part of reef structure, and are often appropriately referred to as the master builders of the reefs. The polyps of the hermatypic (reef-building) corals host a layer of single-celled symbiotic algae (zooxanthellae) just under the surface of their bodies. The algae are highly concentrated within the tissues of the polyps, and by their photosynthesis make a major contribution to the feeding and growth of the corals. Polyps and algae live in a close nutrient exchange relationship. The algae pass most of the energy-rich compounds produced during photosynthesis on to their host polyps, and in return they receive from the polyps compounds containing oxygen and phosphorus, together with the carbon dioxide they need for photosynthesis. Tropical seas are low in nutrients, so this close symbiosis provides the most effective recycling of important nutrients and trace elements. The algae are also very important for the coral's formation of limestone.

## 1 | **Yellow scroll coral** *Turbinaria reniformis*
—Stone corals Dendrophylliidae

**GER**—Gelbe Salatkoralle   I   **FR**—Corail parchemin jaune

**LENGTH**  Diameter 300 cm
**BIOLOGY**  Striking, sulphur-yellow colonies of convoluted, lettuce-like plates. The upper surfaces have a nubbly appearance because of the cone-shaped polyp calyces. Prefers a sunny location.
**DISTRIBUTION**  Red Sea to French Polynesia

## 2 | **Table coral** *Acropora* sp.
—Staghorn corals Acroporidae

**GER**—Tischkoralle   I   **FR**—Corail tabulaire

**LENGTH**  Diameter to more than 200 cm
**BIOLOGY**  Cantilevered growth pattern; horizontal table-like plates made up of lots of finely branched twigs, which can form an almost solid plate. There are several very similar species. Lives on sheltered reef slopes, especially under the edge of the reef and on the uppermost reef slope.
**DISTRIBUTION**  Red Sea to Polynesia

**1** | **Maze coral** *Herpolitha limax*
—Mushroom corals Fungiidae

**GER**—Gabel-Pilzkoralle  I  **FR**—Corail labyrinthe

**LENGTH** 60 cm
**BIOLOGY** In lagoons and on outer reef slopes. Elongated with rounded ends. Frequently also forked. Has several mouths; 2–50 m.
**DISTRIBUTION** Red Sea to French Polynesia

**2** | **Bubble coral** *Plerogyra sinuosa*
—Caryophylliidae

**GER**—Blasenkoralle  I  **FR**—Corail bulles

**LENGTH** Diameter 150 cm
**BIOLOGY** Beige to greyish-green. During the daytime, it is covered with bubbles, which provide the zooxanthellae with the best conditions for photosynthesis. At night, the polyps extend their tentacles to catch plankton; 1–40 m.
**DISTRIBUTION** Red Sea to French Polynesia

**3** | **Stony coral** *Oxypora convoluta*
—Stony corals Lobophylliidae

**GER**—Zahnkoralle  I  **FR**—Corail vinaigrier

**LENGTH** 2 m
**BIOLOGY** On protected reef slopes. Rare species. Curved plates with ragged edges; 1–30 m.
**DISTRIBUTION** Red Sea

**LITTLE THORN CORALS — ANTIPATHIDAE**
Little thorn corals are also known as black corals, although this normally refers to the large, bush-like colonies. However, it is only the axial skeleton that is black, and this is not visible from the outside in living colonies because it is covered by tissue in which the polyps are embedded.
**BLACK JEWELS** The horny black skeleton of some large species has been made into jewellery since ancient times. In some areas, whole branches of the bushy types are also sold as souvenirs. As a result, they are heavily fished in many places and stocks have been badly depleted. In addition, black coral used to be sold as a medicine or lucky charm against illness in Europe, and still is in Asia. This is the origin of its scientific name (*Antipathes* means 'against illness'). The species most commonly seen by divers in the Indo-Pacific are those illustrated here, as well as *Cirrhipathes anguina*. This is very similar to *C. spiralis* but is smaller – less than 100 cm – and less regular.

**1** | **Spiral coral** *Cirrhipathes spiralis*
—Little thorn corals Antipathidae

**GER**—Spiralige Drahtkoralle  I  **FR**—Corail spiralé blanc

**LENGTH** 250 cm
**BIOLOGY** As in the branching black coral, closer inspection reveals the numerous tiny thorns and hooks on the surface, which give the little thorn corals their name. Lives in a location with a strong current, usually below 10 m. The polyps catch plankton that are driven past by the current.
**DISTRIBUTION** Red Sea to western Pacific

**2** | **Branching black coral** *Antipathes dichotoma*
—Little thorn corals Antipathidae

**GER**—Schwarze Drahtkoralle  I  **FR**—Corail noir ramifié

**LENGTH** 300 cm
**BIOLOGY** Prefers steep reef slopes with strong currents; usually below 30 m, but in some places in far shallower water. Grows very slowly: a large colony with a base stem of arm thickness is many decades old. Often colonized by other plankton-feeders such as feather stars, brittle stars and winged oysters. A favourite residence also of Longnose hawkfish.
**DISTRIBUTION** Red Sea to French Polynesia

**BRISTLEWORMS — POLYCHAETA**
There are around 10,000 known species of brittleworm, almost all of which live in the sea. They live in plankton, buried in sand or mud, and also in crevices or moving around freely in rock and coral reefs. There are two distinct groups.
**ON PATROL** Mobile species are mainly predatory feeders and are mostly nocturnal. They eat other worms, crustaceans, non-mobile creatures and detritus. In a few species the bristles are used for defence. They are positioned in dense clumps and can easily penetrate human skin, where they break off; their toxin causes a painful burning sensation.
**SEDENTARY** Other species have given up their mobile lifestyle for a more sedentary one. They specialize in catching plankton, and have developed a crown of tentacles for that purpose; this is normally all that is visible of the worm. The rest of the body is hidden inside a tube it has made and which it will never leave. The *Sabellidae* family lives in tubes that have a rubbery or parchment texture; *Serpulidae* live in limestone tubes.

## 1 | Christmas tree worm *Spirobranchus giganteus*
—Serpulid tubeworms Serpulidae

**GER**—Weihnachtsbaum-Röhrenwurm  I  **FR**—Ver-arbre de Noël

**LENGTH** Diameter 1.5 cm (crown)
**BIOLOGY** Embedded in living coral, often in groups. The crown is made up of two spiral rings of tentacles; colour very variable: white, yellow, orange, blue, dark purple, blackish, sometimes also spotted. Plankton feeder. Very timid, retracts instantly in response to any suspicious shadow or wave movement.
**DISTRIBUTION** Circumtropical

## 2 | Peacock bristleworm *Chloeia flava*
—Fireworms Amphinomidae

**GER**—Gelber Feuerwurm  I  **FR**—Ver de feu paon

**LENGTH** 10 cm
**BIOLOGY** Usually on sand or gravel; regularly seen in coastal areas. Scavenger and predator, is able to swim across the seabed. Broad body with dense tufts of long yellow bristles. Caution: the bristles will cause a burning pain if touched.
**DISTRIBUTION** Red Sea to western Pacific

1

2

**FLATWORMS—PLATYHELMINTHES**

**GLIDERS** Most marine flatworms grow to several centimetres in length, some to more than 10 cm. Several hundred species are already known, but marine biologists regularly discover new ones. Flatworms are the masters of a fast, fluent gliding motion over the seabed, adjusting to any unevenness in the ground. Some of the larger species are able to swim using wave-like movements, but only for short distances.

**A KEEN NOSE** They find their way primarily by scent when searching for food or a mate. To do this, they stretch up their 'heads' at intervals in order to gauge the direction of a scent more accurately.

**SPECIAL DIET** Most species are predators and prefer to feed on non-mobile invertebrates. Many individual species, though, have specialized dietary requirements, and their menu includes sponges, bryozoans and sea squirts, for example. Flatworms are well protected against predators by toxins stored in their bodies, and the vivid patterns on many species are probably intended as a warning sign.

## 1 | Gold-dotted flatworm *Thysanozoon* sp.
—Flatworms Pseudocerotidae

**GER**—Goldregen-Plattwurm  I  **FR**—Ver plat à points dorés

**LENGTH** 5 cm
**BIOLOGY** Relatively common. This species is often seen swimming by means of wave-like movements.
**DISTRIBUTION** Red Sea, many very similar species in the Indo-Pacific

## 2 | Glorious flatworm *Pseudobiceros gloriosus*
—Flatworms Pseudocerotidae

**GER**—Pracht-Plattwurm  I  **FR**—Ver plat glorieux

**LENGTH** 9 cm
**BIOLOGY** Many very similar species with marginal edges in different colour combinations. Is able to swim; mainly nocturnal.
**DISTRIBUTION** Red Sea to Hawaii

1
2

**1** | **Susan's flatworm** *Pseudoceros susanae*
—Flatworms Pseudocerotidae

**GER**—Susans Plattwurm  I  **FR**—Ver plat de Susan

**LENGTH**  3 cm
**BIOLOGY**  Centre back orange with white longitudinal stripe. Margin usually purplish violet. Usually on hard substrates, locally fairly frequent.
**DISTRIBUTION**  Central Indian Ocean (Maldives, Seychelles) to Indonesia, the Philippines

**2** | **Fuchsia flatworm** *Pseudoceros* cf. *ferrugineus*
—Flatworms Pseudocerotidae

**GER**—Rost-Plattwurm  I  **FR**—Ver plat fuchsia

**LENGTH**  5 cm
**BIOLOGY**  Background colour rusty red to scarlet, with a dense sprinkling of small white spots. Feeds on colony-forming sea squirts, active by both day and night.
**DISTRIBUTION**  Red Sea to Polynesia

**3** | **Bedford's flatworm** *Pseudobiceros bedfordi*
—Flatworms Pseudocerotidae

**GER**—Bedfords Plattwurm  I  **FR**—Ver plat de Bedford

**LENGTH**  10 cm
**BIOLOGY**  A large, eye-catching species in a variety of strong, intense colourings. Can glide across the seabed very quickly, and is an elegant swimmer. Its diet includes sea squirts.
**DISTRIBUTION**  Red Sea to western Pacific

1
2
3

## 1 | Orsak's flatworm *Maiazoon orsaki*
—Flatworms Pseudocerotidae

**GER**—Karamell-Plattwurm  I  **FR**—Ver plat d'Orsak

**LENGTH** 6 cm
**BIOLOGY** Cream-coloured with a brown ruffled edge tipped with black. Its small eyespot is visible in the middle of its head. The photo shows it on a colony of sea squirts, one of its food sources.
**DISTRIBUTION** Indo-Pacific

## 2 | Racing stripe flatworm *Pseudoceros bifurcus*
—Flatworms Pseudocerotidae

**GER**—Rennstreifen-Plattwurm  I  **FR**—Ver plat à rayure

**LENGTH** 6 cm
**BIOLOGY** Blue or purple with a white central stripe. This has dark marginal lines and a longitudinal orange patch at the front. On hard substrates, not rare.
**DISTRIBUTION** Indo-West Pacific

## 3 | Linda's flatworm *Pseudoceros lindae*
—Flatworms Pseudocerotidae

**GER**—Lindas Plattwurm  I  **FR**—Ver plat de Linda

**LENGTH** 5 cm
**BIOLOGY** Reddish-brown with orange spots, these usually yellowish to white towards the margin. On sand and hard substrates.
**DISTRIBUTION** Indo-West Pacific

# Prosobranch Snails

**PROSOBRANCH SNAILS—PROSOBRANCHIA**
Snails are the largest group of molluscs, with more than 110,000 species.
Most are shelled snails, i.e. they have a protective shell.
**GRAZER** A typical feature of snails is their highly developed rasping tongue
(radula). This carries many minute teeth, enabling the snail to graze algae
from surfaces. In doing this they also eat numerous invertebrates, and some
are able to use a drilling action to make circular holes in the shells of other
snails or molluscs. Some, like the cone snail, have highly modified tongues.
**VENOMOUS ARROWS** All cone snails are active hunters able to catch even
agile fish. That proverbially slow snails are able to do this is a remarkable
natural development. Cone snails hunt with venomous arrows, and their
venom is one of the most powerful known: some types can kill a person
very quickly. However, humans are only in danger if they collect or handle
them. For safety's sake, cone snails should never be touched.

## 1 | Triton's trumpet *Charonia tritonis* —Tritons Ranellidae

**GER**—Tritonshorn  |  **FR**—Triton géant

**LENGTH** 50 cm
**BIOLOGY** A nocturnal predator, hunts large starfish, including crown-of-
thorns starfish. Uses sulphuric acid to dissolve the shells of sea urchins.
**DISTRIBUTION** Red Sea to Polynesia; Mediterranean

## 2 | Umbilical ovula *Calpurnus verrucosus* —Ovulids Ovulidae

**GER**—Nabel-Eischnecke  |  **FR**—Ovule-ongle

**LENGTH** 4.5 cm
**BIOLOGY** Feeds mainly on *Sarcophyton* and *Lobophyton* soft corals (see
p. 194), also on sponges.
**DISTRIBUTION** Red Sea to Fiji

## 3 | Textile cone shell *Conus textile* —Cones Conidae

**GER**—Textil-Kegelschnecke  |  **FR**—Cône drap d'or

**LENGTH** 15 cm
**BIOLOGY** Nocturnal, feeds on snails and cone snails, worms and fish.
Extremely dangerous. Lives up to nine years.
**DISTRIBUTION** Red Sea to French Polynesia

1
2
3

## SEA SLUGS—NUDIBRANCHIA

Sea slugs grow very quickly. Most species live only a few months, and the few that live as long as a year are almost Methuselahs. During their short lives some species grow to between 1 cm and 10 cm; few grow larger than this. Sea slugs have an ingenious defence system, and are fond of eating poisonous prey. These two facts are connected: many non-mobile animals such as sponges, cnidarians and sea squirts are protected against predators by toxins in their tissues. Most sea slug species, however, have developed their feeding habits to specialize in eating these non-mobile creatures.

**POISON RESERVOIR**  They are immune to the poison of their prey, and even store the venomous substances in their own tissues, thus themselves becoming poisonous and therefore protected against predators. Shag-rug snails eat cnidarians and store the latter's poison capsules in their own dorsal appendages for their own protection. Some also take over the symbiotic algae (zooxanthellae) of their prey.

### 1 | Purple nudibranch *Nembrotha purpureolineata* —Sea slugs Polyceridae

**GER**—Gestreifte Nembrota  I  **FR**—Nembrotha à lignes pourpres

**LENGTH**  6 cm
**BIOLOGY**  Like other *Nembrotha* slugs this is noted for rapid crawling and responsive locomotion.
**DISTRIBUTION**  East Africa to Japan and western Australia

### 2 | Pyjama nudibranch *Chromodoris quadricolor* Colourful sea slugs Chromodorididae

**GER**—Pyjama-Sternschnecke  I  **FR**—Doris-pyjama

**LENGTH**  4.5 cm
**BIOLOGY**  One of the Red Sea's commonest and most familiar species. Feeds on the Red Sea sponge (see p. 186).
**DISTRIBUTION**  Red Sea to Tanzania

### 3 | Triton's nudibranch *Risbecia tryoni* —Colourful sea slugs Chromodorididae

**GER**—Tryons-Sternschnecke  I  **FR**—Risbécie de Tryon

**LENGTH**  10 cm
**BIOLOGY**  Frequently prowls around in pairs in single file, the slug at the back using its head to maintain contact with the one at the front.
**DISTRIBUTION**  East Africa to French Polynesia

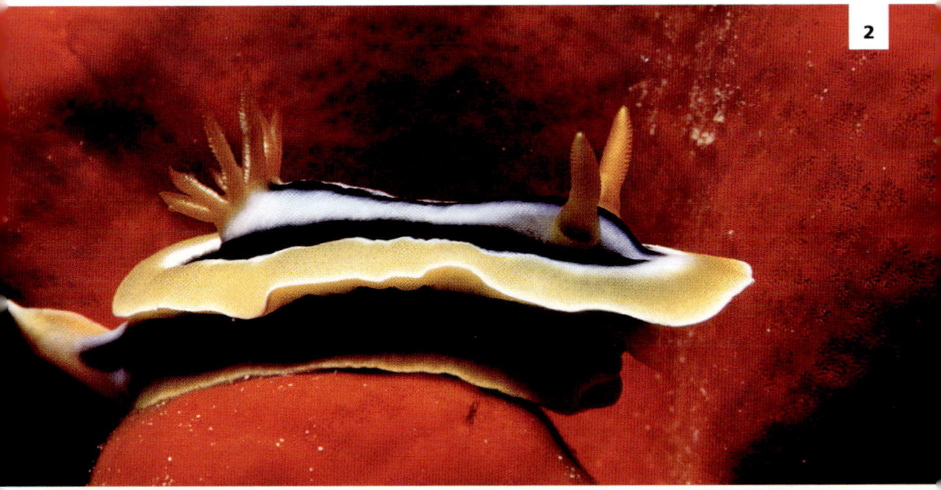

**1** | **Spanish dancer** *Hexabranchus sanguineus*
—Spanish dancers Hexabranchidae

**GER**—Spanische Tänzerin  |  **FR**—Danseuse espagnole

**LENGTH** up to 50 cm
**BIOLOGY** One of the largest species, and can swim in spectacular fashion using elegant wave-like movements. Scarlet in the Red Sea (see photograph), mostly 'only' 30 cm long. Orange or yellow in other places.
**DISTRIBUTION** Red Sea to French Polynesia

**2** | **Kune's chromodoris** *Chromodoris kuniei*
—Colourful sea slugs Chromodorididae

**GER**—Kunie-Sternschnecke  |  **FR**—Doris de Kunié

**LENGTH** 5 cm
**BIOLOGY** Common, feeds on sponges. There are at least two very similar species in the Indo-Pacific that differ in their colour patterning (*C. geminus* and *C. tritos*).
**DISTRIBUTION** Indonesia to Australia, the Philippines and Marshall Islands

**3** | **Eyespot nudibranch** *Phyllidia ocellata*
—Dorid sea slugs Phyllidiidae

**GER**—Augenflecken-Warzenschnecke  |  **FR**—Phyllidie ocellée

**LENGTH** 6 cm
**BIOLOGY** A common species with many colour variants; *P. undula* (Red Sea) has black-and-white, wave-like stripes, and may itself be only a variant. Feeds on sponges.
**DISTRIBUTION** Red Sea, Indian Ocean to western Pacific

# Sea Slugs

**1** | **Serpent pteraeolidia** *Pteraeolidia ianthina*
—Aeolid nudibranchs Facelinidae

**GER**—Blauer Drache  |  **FR**—Pteraeolidie mauve

**LENGTH** 10 cm
**BIOLOGY** Colour variable: green, blue or purple, depending on the algae in its tissues. Eats cnidarians such as sea fern and leather coral, adopting their stinging capsules and symbiotic algae.
**DISTRIBUTION** Red Sea to French Polynesia

**2** | **Robe-hem hypselodoris** *Hypselodoris apolegma*
—Colurful sea slugs Chromodorididae

**GER**—Purpur-Sternschnecke  |  **FR**—Doris ourlée

**LENGTH** 10 cm
**BIOLOGY** Locally relatively common. On hard substrates. There are other very similar species, so only recognized as a separate species a few years ago.
**DISTRIBUTION** From Malaysia and Indonesia to the Philippines and Japan

**3** | **Swollen phyllidia** *Phyllidia varicosa*
—Dorid sea slugs Phyllidiidae

**GER**—Variable Warzenschnecke  |  **FR**—Phyllidie verruqueuse

**LENGTH** 11 cm
**BIOLOGY** Widely distributed and very common species. Crawls mostly over coral rock but also over pebbles. Feeds on sponges.
**DISTRIBUTION** Red Sea and East Africa to Japan, Palau and the Society Islands

1
2
3

BIVALVES—BIVALVIA
Like snails and cephalopods, bivalves belong to the mollusc group
(Mollusca). Most bivalves are active filter feeders. They take in water
through a breathing aperture and eject it through an outlet opening, at the
same time filtering out plankton as the water passes over the gills. Some
species, such as the giant clam, have symbiotic algae, which supply them
with additional nutrients from photosynthesis.
**SKIPPERS** Most species burrow in the sand, while others fasten themselves
to hard surfaces by means of byssal threads. Some bore into rock or coral
branches. Fileshell mussels can swim short distances when threatened,
using a 'skipping' motion by clapping the two parts of their shell together.
**SENSITIVE PEARLS** Some molluscs produce pearls by covering an
introduced irritant, such as a grain of sand, with layers of mother of pearl.
Some species have rows of simple eyes on the edge of the outer shell, and
also sensory cells that react to pressure waves: the thorny oyster, for
example, will snap its shell closed instantly if a diver approaches carelessly.

## 1 | Squamose giant clam *Tridacna squamosa*
—Giant clams Tridacnidae

**GER**—Schuppige Riesenmuschel  |  **FR**—Grand bénitier gaufré

**LENGTH** 40 cm
**BIOLOGY** A thick, wavy shell with deeply convoluted, widely separated
scales. The outer shell is usually greyish-blue, green or brownish. Mostly
more or less firmly embedded in crevices, or grown into coral blocks. Feeds
mainly on the photosynthesis products made by its zooxanthellae. Closes
its shell relatively slowly when disturbed.
**DISTRIBUTION** Red Sea to Samoa

## 2 | Orange-mouth thorny oyster *Spondylus varius*
—Spondylus Spondylidae

**GER**—Variable Stachelauster  |  **FR**—Spondyle variable

**LENGTH** 25 cm
**BIOLOGY** Shell is always covered with algae, sponges and other
colonizers. Outer shell very colourful and variable: yellow, orange, red,
blue and lilac markings, and rows of small eyes on the upper and lower
edges. Closes its shell immediately and very quickly at the slightest
disturbance.
**DISTRIBUTION** Red Sea to Marshall Islands

1

2

**OCTOPUSES — OCTOPODIDAE**
All members of the octopus family are typical bottom-dwellers, but octopuses are able to swim, although they rarely do so. They swim using a jet-propulsion method, expelling water through their movable breathing siphon. The octopus can change colour within a fraction of a second to camouflage itself against its background.

**1** | **Day octopus** *Octopus cyanea*
—Octopuses Octopodidae

**GER**—Roter Krake | **FR**—Poulpe de récif commun

**LENGTH** 100 cm
**BIOLOGY** The most common species seen by divers on Indo-Pacific coral reefs. Active by day also. Lives in lagoons and outer reef slopes, from the shallows down to more than 25 m. Uses small caves or crevices as a burrow, frequently reducing the size of the entrance with molluscs and stones. Eats mainly prawns, sometimes also molluscs and fish.
**DISTRIBUTION** Red Sea to Polynesia

**CUTTLEFISHES — SEPIIDAE**
Cuttlefishes can change instantly to a variety of different colour patterns. They have eight arms, plus two longer tentacles covered with suckers, which they throw out far in front of them to catch their prey. Although cuttlefish live on the seabed, they often swim or hover slightly above the ground.

**2** | **Pharaoh cuttlefish** *Sepia pharaonis*
—Cuttlefishes Sepiidae

**GER**—Pharao-Sepia | **FR**—Seiche pharaon

**LENGTH** 40 cm (body)
**BIOLOGY** Can change not only its colour but also the structure of its skin, using muscle contractions to form ragged protuberances and flaps on its normally smooth skin. When disturbed, and also during the breeding season, it has distinct horizontal stripes. Frequently swims at night in shallow water, feeds on crustaceans and fish; 0.3–110 m.
**DISTRIBUTION** Red Sea to Japan

1

2

CRUSTACEANS—CRUSTACEA

**KNIGHTS OF THE SEA** About 45,000 species of crustacean have been recorded, but there could be many more, since new ones are constantly being discovered. Crustaceans have been wearing suits of armour for more than 500 million years. With many developments and variations, the basic principle is still the same: a movable exoskeleton that covers the animal completely. Despite their armour, crustaceans are highly mobile and agile, as their protection is made of chitin, which is both hard and lightweight.

**NEW ARMOUR** An exoskeleton has a major drawback, however: it does not get bigger as its wearer grows. It has to be replaced at intervals when a growth spurt is due to take place. This is when crustaceans moult. The new armour is formed underneath the old one before the latter is shed. Once the creature has worked its way out of the old shell, which is now too small, it can make a sudden growth spurt because the new shell is still soft and flexible. Some species can grow up to 30 per cent in length at each moult.

**1** | **Harlequin shrimp** *Hymenocera elegans*
—Harlequin shrimps Hymenoceridae

**GER**—Harlekin-Garnele  |  **FR**—Crevette Arlequin

**LENGTH** 5 cm
**BIOLOGY** Usually lives in a pair with a territory, a permanent bond that can last for years. The bond is ensured by a pheromone produced by the female. They cooperate to turn starfish upside down, and then they eat their feet and viscera.
**DISTRIBUTION** Red Sea to Indonesia

**2** | **Banded coral shrimp** *Stenopus hispidus*
—Decapods Stenopodidae

**GER**—Gebänderte Scherengarnele  |  **FR**—Grande crevette nettoyeuse

**LENGTH** 5 cm
**BIOLOGY** Usually lives in crevices, sometimes in pairs; males are smaller than females. They maintain cleaning stations, enticing client fish to their shelters by waving their antennae. Cleaning symbiosis benefits both parties: the fish have their skin parasites removed and the shrimps get a meal.
**DISTRIBUTION** Circumtropical

1
2

**1** | **Painted spiny lobster** *Panulirus versicolor*
—Spiny lobsters Palinuridae

**GER**—Gestreifte Languste | **FR**—Langouste peinte

**LENGTH** 40 cm
**BIOLOGY** Spends the day in crevices, often with its long antennae protruding. Sociable, frequently in small groups. Prowls the reef at night, eating molluscs, starfish, worms and dead fish; 1 m to at least 50 m.
**DISTRIBUTION** Red Sea to French Polynesia

**2** | **Clam digger** *Scyllarides tridacnophaga*
—Slipper lobsters Scyllaridae

**GER**—Muschel-Bärenkrebs | **FR**—Cigale honteuse

**LENGTH** 35 cm
**BIOLOGY** Nocturnal. Able to open giant clams and dig out prey from soft ground using its plate-like antennae. When threatened, moves quickly away backwards by collapsing its tail sections; 1–122 m.
**DISTRIBUTION** Red Sea to Thailand

**3** | **Anemone hermit crab** *Dardanus pedunculatus*
—Hermit crabs Diogenidae

**GER**—Anemonen-Einsiedler | **FR**—Bernard-l'ermite à yeux verts

**LENGTH** 10 cm
**BIOLOGY** Nocturnal, predatory omnivore. Almost always lives in symbiosis with an anemone, which it takes with it when moving to a new housing.
**DISTRIBUTION** East Africa, Maldives to French Polynesia

**1** | **Porcelain anemone crab** *Neopetrolisthes oshima*
—Porcelain crabs Porcellanidae

**GER**—Gefleckter Porzellankrebs  |  **FR**—Crabe porcelaine d'anémone

**LENGTH**  2.5 cm
**BIOLOGY**  Almost invariably lives in pairs on sea anemones. Feeds by filtration, waving around its third pair of gnathopods, which have long, fine bristles.
**DISTRIBUTION**  Indo- and western Pacific

**2** | **Red reef crab** *Carpilius convexus*
—Reef crabs Carpiliidae

**GER**—Konvexe Riffkrabbe  |  **FR**—Crabe rouge du corail

**LENGTH**  9 cm
**BIOLOGY**  Colour variable: uniform orange-red to reddish-brown, or marbled. Lives on reef tops and slopes. Feeds at night on snails and sea urchins, opens shells with its powerful claws.
**DISTRIBUTION**  Red Sea to French Polynesia

**3** | **Harlequin crab** *Lissocarcinus orbicularis*
—Xanthid crabs Xanthidae

**GER**—Harlekin-Schwimmkrabbe  |  **FR**—Crabe arlequin

**LENGTH**  4 cm
**BIOLOGY**  Colour variable: dark brown to orange pattern on a white background, or vice versa. Often on sea cucumbers, on which they live commensally; timid, often remains on underside of cucumber during the day.
**DISTRIBUTION**  Red Sea to Fiji

**1** | **Dancing shrimp** *Rhynchocinetes durbanensis*
—Dancing shrimps Rhynchocinetidae

**GER**—Durban Tanzgarnele  |  **FR**—Crevette danseuse de Durban

**LENGTH** 18 cm
**BIOLOGY** Raptorial forelegs with club-shaped swelling for breaking up hard-shelled prey. Inhabits U-shaped tubes, which it retreats to if disturbed, but can also be inquisitive and fearless.
**DISTRIBUTION** East Africa, Maldives to Samoa

**2** | **Wire coral crab** *Xenocarcinus tuberculatus*
—Wire coral crabs Epialtidae

**GER**—Drahtkorallen-Spinnenkrabbe  |  **FR**—Crabe-araignée de corail-fouet

**LENGTH** 18 cm
**BIOLOGY** Lives commensally on wire corals (*Cirrhipathes* spp.), often matching the colour and texture of its host. Its elongated body and cryptic patterning provide camouflage among the coral's branches. Typically solitary and sedentary, it clings tightly to the coral and is rarely seen away from it.
**DISTRIBUTION** East Africa, Maldives to Samoa

**3** | **Peacock mantis shrimp** *Odontodactylus scyllarus*
—Mantis shrimps Odontodactylidae

**GER**—Harlekin-Fangschreckenkrebs  |  **FR**—Squille multicolore

**LENGTH** 18 cm
**BIOLOGY** Raptorial legs with long spines for impaling its prey. Black, green, yellow, white, sometimes patterned. Can adapt its colour to a new environment within months.
**DISTRIBUTION** East Africa, Maldives to Samoa

**FEATHER STARS — CRINOIDEA**
Feather stars have very flexible arms and are often brightly coloured. They are able to move and hold themselves in position by the claw-like cilia on their undersides. Some hide in crevices during the day and climb up at night to exposed positions on the reef, where they stretch out their arms to catch plankton in the current.

**1** | **Variable bushy feather star** *Comanthina schlegelii* —Feather stars Comatulidae

**GER**—Schlegels Haarstern  |  **FR**—Comatule buissonneuse variable

**LENGTH** 20 cm
**BIOLOGY** Very common. Colour very variable: sometimes a uniform colour, sometimes arms and pinna are a different colour. Has up to 130 closely packed arms. Can be seen in the daytime also, on exposed locations with strong currents. It often holds itself in position not only with its cilia but also with its lower, and often shorter, arms.
**DISTRIBUTION** Maldives to western Pacific

**BRITTLE STARS — OPHIUROIDEA**
With 2,000 species, the brittle stars are the largest group of the echinoderm genus, which also includes feather stars, starfish, sea urchins and sea cucumbers. They hide in crevices, under stones or in soft ground during the day, and emerge at night, when they graze detritus from the ground or catch plankton from the water.

**2** | **Long-spined brittle star** *Ophiothrix savignyi* —Brittle stars Ophiotrichidae

**GER**—Savignys Schlangenstern  |  **FR**—Ophiure à longues épines

**LENGTH** 15 cm
**BIOLOGY** Their flexible arms make brittle stars highly mobile and relatively fast: they are the sprinters of their genus. They crawl by bending and stretching their arms forwards. The arms are easily broken off; if a predator grabs one of them, it can snap off at any point, allowing the brittle star to escape.
**DISTRIBUTION** Red Sea to New Caledonia

1

2

STARFISH—ASTEROIDEA
Around 1,600 species are known, varying in diameter from less than 1 cm to more than 100 cm. Most have five arms but some species have more. They move by means of the numerous small feet – there can be several hundred to over a thousand – on the underside of their bodies; the arms themselves hardly move at all.

**INVERTIBLE STOMACH** Many species are predators, but they also eat carrion. Their prey include a wide range of invertebrates including sponges, crustaceans, snails, molluscs, bryozoa, sea squirts, and also other starfish. Many species are not choosy and will eat whatever they find and are able to overpower. Starfish have a mouth located on the underside (oral surface); they evert their stomach through it to feed. If the prey is too large, it is pre-digested outside the starfish's body, and then eaten in liquefied form.

**REGENERATORS** Many species are able to fully regenerate missing arms. Some, especially the *Linckia* species, reproduce asexually by breaking off one of their own arms, which will eventually grow into a complete starfish.

## 1 | **Blue sea star** *Linckia laevigata* —Sea stars Ophidiasteridae

**GER**—Blauer Seestern | **FR**—Étoile de mer bleue

**LENGTH** 40 cm
**BIOLOGY** Can break off one of its own arms, which will then grow into a complete animal.
**DISTRIBUTION** East Africa, Indo-Pacific to Hawaii

## 2 | **Granulated sea star** *Choriaster granulatus* —Sea stars Oreasteridae

**GER**—Walzenstern | **FR**—Étoile de mer granuleuse

**LENGTH** 25 cm
**BIOLOGY** Colour variable: white, cream, orange to red. Lives on hard surfaces and living coral, feeds on detritus and small invertebrates.
**DISTRIBUTION** Red Sea to Fiji

## 3 | **Crown-of-thorns starfish** *Acanthaster planci* —Crown-of-thorns starfish Acanthasteridae

**GER**—Dornenkrone | **FR**—Étoile de mer à couronne d'épines

**LENGTH** 50 cm
**BIOLOGY** Feeds on the polyps of stone coral. When present in large numbers, can damage large areas of reef. Caution: spines are venomous.
**DISTRIBUTION** Red Sea to Mexico

1
2 
3

**SEA URCHINS—ECHINOIDEA**
Sea urchins are mainly nocturnal, and many species spend the day hidden in holes and crevices on the reef. Others, like Diadematidae, sometimes also rest in an open area, but crowded closely together in a large group for protection. Despite their largely defensive cluster of spines, sea urchins have predators, including various triggerfish, pufferfish and wrasses. Their nocturnal lifestyle is therefore regarded as a form of protective behaviour.
**GRAZING** Sea urchins feed primarily on minute algae, which they scrape off rocks. Depending on species, some of them also eat, to some extent, a variety of non-mobile creatures, including coral polyps.
**SHARP SPINES** There are about 900 species worldwide. Many of them have spines that are sharp, and in the case of the diadem urchins, very long – more than 40 cm. Other species have very short or blunt spines. The slate pencil urchin, for example, has spines that are the thickness of a pencil and the length of a finger, but blunt. They use them to wedge themselves firmly in crevices at night.

**1** | **Globe urchin** *Mespillia globulus*
—Sea urchins Temnopleuridae

**GER**—Kugel-Seeigel  |  **FR**—Oursin globe

**LENGTH** 5 cm
**BIOLOGY** The colour of the five broad bands without spines can vary from blue to green shades. Scrapes algae from hard surfaces. Camouflages itself with algae and fragments of coral and shell. More common at night, but not an unusual sight during the day out in the open.
**DISTRIBUTION** India, Maldives to western Pacific

**2** | **Hatpin urchin** *Echinothrix calamaris*
—Diadem sea urchins Diadematidae

**GER**—Calamaris-Seeigel  |  **FR**—Oursin épingle

**LENGTH** 20 cm
**BIOLOGY** The long spines are striped in juveniles (see photograph), but in adults are usually black, very occasionally white. The spines can easily penetrate human skin and are very painful; 1–30 m.
**DISTRIBUTION** Red Sea to Hawaii and Pitcairn Islands

**1** | **Fire urchin** *Asthenosoma varium*
—Fire urchins Echinothuridae

**GER**—Variabler Feuerseeigel  |  **FR**—Oursin de feu variable

**LENGTH**  28 cm
**BIOLOGY**  Usually hides during the day, tends to be active at night, out in the open. It often has commensal shrimps or prawns living on its surface. The spines can cause very painful injuries; 1–285 m.
**DISTRIBUTION**  Oman to New Caledonia

**2** | **Rousseau's urchin** *Microcyphus rousseaui*
—Sea urchins Temnopleuridae

**GER**—Rousseaus Seeigel  |  **FR**—Oursin de Rousseau

**LENGTH**  5 cm
**BIOLOGY**  The areas without spines have a striking zigzag pattern. Scrapes algal growth and non-mobile animals from hard surfaces. A rare species, nocturnal; 1–30 m.
**DISTRIBUTION**  Red Sea, Gulf of Oman to southern Mozambique

**3** | **Slate pencil urchin** *Heterocentrotus mamillatus*
—Sea urchins Echinometridae

**GER**—Griffel-Seeigel  |  **FR**—Oursin crayon

**LENGTH**  30 cm
**BIOLOGY**  Has thick, blunt primary spines with a white ring at the base. Uses them to wedge itself into holes and crevices during the day. A nocturnal omnivore, often in shallow areas between 0.5 m and 10 m.
**DISTRIBUTION**  Red Sea to Polynesia

**SEA CUCUMBERS—HOLOTHUROIDEA**
More than 1,200 species are known worldwide, from the polar regions to the tropics and from tidal zones to the deepest oceans. They range in size from 1 cm to more than 200 cm. On Indo-Pacific reefs, the large numbers of sea cucumbers on hard ground and sand are a familiar sight. Despite their appearance, sea cucumbers are echinoderms just like starfish, sea urchins, brittle stars and feather stars.
**DEBRIS FEEDER**  Most of the sea cucumbers that live on reefs feed by swallowing large quantities of sand from the upper layers and utilizing the organic material (detritus) that it contains. Some species live mainly on hard surfaces, and pick up debris from the surface using the shield-like ends of their tentacles; this behaviour can often be seen by observing the leopard sea cucumber. Yet other species have bushy tentacles and feed on plankton. They stretch their crown of tentacles out into open water in order to catch passing zooplankton and organic particles.
**STICKY THREADS**  Some species release long, sticky and slightly poisonous threads if disturbed.

**1** | **Weight watcher** *Holothuria fuscogilva*
—Sea cucumbers Holothuridae

**GER**—Edel-Seegurke  I  **FR**—Holothurie noble

**LENGTH**  50 cm
**BIOLOGY**  Sand and reefs. Feeds on debris and minute animals. A valued species in Asia, where it is known as the 'trepang'.
**DISTRIBUTION**  Red Sea to French Polynesia

**2** | **Leopard sea cucumber** *Pearsonothuria graeffei*
—Sea cucumbers Holothuriidae

**GER**—Gestrichelte Seegurke  I  **FR**—Holothurie léopard

**LENGTH**  50 cm
**BIOLOGY**  On rock and coral reefs; a good climber. Picks up debris using its flattened tentacles.
**DISTRIBUTION**  Red Sea to French Polynesia

**3** | **Sea apple** *Pseudocolochirus violaceus*
—Sea cucumbers Holothuridae

**GER**—Apfel-Seegurke  I  **FR**—Pomme de mer

**LENGTH**  15 cm
**BIOLOGY**  Uses its bushy tentacles to catch plankton and detritus. Colours vary: yellow, blue and red. Frequently in groups.
**DISTRIBUTION**  Indonesia to the Philippines

**SEA SQUIRTS—ASCIDIACEA**
**AMALGAMATION** There are solitary, social and colony-forming species of
sea squirt. The social types live in small groups and are joined only at the
base. Colony-forming species can be made up of many thousands of mini-
individuals whose outer covering has amalgamated to form a single mass.
**PUMPING STATION** Sea squirts are small but high-performance pumps.
They are active filter-feeders on organic particles and micro-organisms in
the water around them. To feed, they pump large volumes of water
through their bodies; some species that have been studied achieved a pump
output of around 175 litres per day.
**FINE-GAUGE FILTER** The water flows through a branchial basket that
makes up most of the inside of a sea squirt and acts as a filter bag. Even the
most minute particles of 0.0005 mm are retained. The entire system is self-
cleaning: at intervals, sea squirts draw themselves together and force water
back out through the inlet openings. Any unwanted matter is ejected from
the gullet, which is thus cleaned.

**1** | **Blue tunicate** *Rhopalaea crassa*
—Sea squirts Diazonidae

**GER**—Blaue Seescheide  I  **FR**—Ascidie bleue

**LENGTH** 6 cm
**BIOLOGY** Blue to turquoise, sometimes with a translucent network
pattern. Solitary, often in loose groups.
**DISTRIBUTION** Indonesia to Australia

**2** | **Purple sea squirt** *Polycarpa aurata*
—Sea squirts Styelidae

**GER**—Gold-Seescheide  I  **FR**—Ascidie dorée

**LENGTH** 10 cm
**BIOLOGY** Solitary, a common and widespread species. Only reproduces
sexually. Closes its openings if disturbed.
**DISTRIBUTION** Sri Lanka to Micronesia

**3** | **Robust sea squirt** *Atriolum robustum*
—Sea squirts Didemnidae

**GER**—Robuste Seescheide  I  **FR**—Ascidie robuste

**LENGTH** 3 cm
**BIOLOGY** Colony-forming: each of the small inlet openings represents
one individual, and they all share one large outlet opening.
**DISTRIBUTION** Indonesia to western Pacific

Mediterranean Sea
China
Egypt
Red Sea
India
Arabian Sea
Gulf of Aden
Andaman Islands
Thailand
Lakshadweep
Africa
Malaysia
Kenya
Maldives
Indone
Chagos Archipelago
Seychelles
Cocos (Keeling) Islands
Christmas Is.
Madagascar
Mauritius
INDIAN
OCEAN

Japan
Guam
Hawaii
PACIFIC OCEAN
Marshall Islands
Solomon Islands
Equator
Papua New Guinea
Samoa
French Polynesia
Tuamotu Archipelago
Fiji
Tahiti
Tonga
Cook Islands
New Caledonia
New Zealand
0
1000
2000
3000
KILOMETRES

# Index

# Photo credits/imprint

Inside photos by Manuela Kirschner and Matthias Bergbauer

Front cover: Zebra lyretail angelfish © Manuela Kirschner
Map of tropical marine regions by Wolfgang Lang

This edition first published in the United Kingdom in 2026
by John Beaufoy Publishing Limited,
11 Blenheim Court, 316 Woodstock Road, Oxford OX2 7NS, UK
www.johnbeaufoy.com

10 9 8 7 6 5 4 3 2 1



The information given in this book has been carefully researched and checked, but
the publishers cannot accept any liability. The planning and carrying out of dives are
the sole responsibility of divers themselves. There is no warranty on the part of the
authors, publishers or any persons commissioned by them.

ISBN 9781912081332

Editor of German edition: Monika Weymann
Editor of English edition: Lucy Doncaster
Cover design and original layout and typesetting: Populärgrafik Stuttgart
Design of German edition: Populärgrafik
Design of English edition: Gulmohur

Printed and bound in Malaysia by Times Offset (M) Sdn. Bhd.

# Notes

# Notes